6.30.59
Fugitive Kind" at Milton

To my friends Ellen-Jo & Marty
Best wishes 64   Doug Kingman

KmGmn

Marty Jurow Seein' Stars

Marty Jurow Seein' Stars

A SHOW BIZ ODYSSEY

MARTIN JUROW
as told to Philip Wuntch

SOUTHERN METHODIST UNIVERSITY PRESS
Dallas

Requests for permission to reproduce material from this work should be sent to:
    Rights and Permissions
    Southern Methodist University Press
    PO Box 750415
    Dallas, Texas 75275-0415

LIBRARY OF CONGRESS CATALOGING-IN-PUBLICATION DATA

Jurow, Martin.

    Marty Jurow seein' stars : a show biz odyssey / by Martin Jurow as told to Philip Wuntch.—1st ed.
        p.   cm.
    Includes index
    ISBN 0-87074-461-5 (alk. paper)
    1. Jurow, Martin. 2. Motion picture producers and directors—United States—Biography.
    I. Wuntch, Philip. II. Title.
    PN1998.3.J89 A3 2001
    791.43'0232'092—dc21
    [B]   2001031064

Except where otherwise credited, all photographs are from Martin Jurow's personal collection.

Jacket photograph: Martin Jurow and Natalie Wood on the set of *The Great Race*, Paris, 1962, by Bob Willoughby

Endsheet illustrations: Dong Kingman, c. 1959, watercolor on paper. Collection of Martin and Erin-Jo Jurow

Jacket and text design: Tom Dawson Graphic Design

Printed in the United States of America on acid-free paper

10   9   8   7   6   5   4   3   2   1

For our daughter Erin Jurow
and our grandson
William Guinn Eliscu

ACKNOWLEDGMENTS

WE WOULD LIKE TO THANK the following members of the team:

Our beloved daughter, Erin Jurow, who, when our lights were dimming, stepped in to take control with superior results.

Our beloved grandson, William Guinn Eliscu (Will), who has demonstrated a talent in the arts to mark his entry into the movie world.

My brother, Irving, and his wife, Mae, who established the permanent award for achievement in theatrical excellence in my name at my alma mater, the College of William and Mary. Irving was the classic "Big Brother," who inspired me, guided me and offered quiet approval when needed.

Our friend and collaborator Philip Wuntch, the sole author of my story. Without his retentive powers and infinite patience during five years of effort, this book could never have been written.

His wife, Mimi, deserves my gratitude for her unselfish sacrifice of all those Sunday afternoons she gave to the book.

Our friend Ruth Collins Sharp Altshuler, an irreplaceable and dear member of the team: civic leader, philanthropist and the first female chair of the Southern Methodist University Board of Trustees. She is a woman of diverse interests, un-limited enthusiasm and enormous compassion.

Keith Gregory, Kathryn Lang, Freddie Jane Goff, and Tom Dawson of Southern Methodist University Press, giants of support in bringing our work to completion.

In 1971 we came to Dallas at the urging of my Harvard Law School classmate George Ray. The opportunities he outlined for us were realized year by year. His friendship proved paramount in our start of a new life.

MARTIN JUROW

MANY PEOPLE HAVE BEEN helpful and supportive in the writing of this book. Above all, there is my wife, Mimi—my muse, my great love and the best movie date in the world. I wish to thank my friends at *The Dallas Morning News* for their encouragement; Wendy Rains's dedicated research was of immeasurable help. And, finally, I want to thank anyone who has simply looked forward to going to the movies. This book is for them.

PHILIP WUNTCH

CONTENTS

CHRONOLOGY OF MARTIN JUROW'S LIFE AND CAREER

December 14, 1911
Born in Brooklyn, New York, to Helena
Nachman and Benjamin Jurow.

1928
One semester Washington Square College of
New York University, sponsored by Dean J. B.
Munn. Transferred to the College of William
and Mary, Williamsburg, Virginia.

1932
Graduated William and Mary and entered
Harvard Law School, Cambridge, Massachusetts.

1935
Graduated Harvard Law School and passed
New York bar exam.

1936
Joined New York City law firm of Nathan
Burkan, prominent entertainment attorney and
Tammany leader.

1937
As company manager for George Abbott,
producer of Broadway hits, toured the country
as youngest manager in the business.

1940
Agent for Music Corporation of America, known
as MCA. Head of east coast motion picture and
theatre department.

April, 1942
Married Erin-Jo Guinn. Left MCA to become
east coast talent chief for Warner Bros.

1943
Moved to Los Angeles as assistant to Jack Warner
and Steve Trilling.

1944
Became executive assistant to Hal Wallis.

1948
Daughter Erin born. Became general manager
at Enterprise Studios.

1949
Joined Jimmy Saphier Agency.

1950
Brief stay at Universal Studios preparing for first
personal film effort. Call from William Morris
Agency to move to New York City as eastern
head of motion pictures, theatre, and dramatic
television.

1957
Became executive assistant to Harry Cohn,
Columbia Pictures in Los Angeles.

1958
Jurow-Shepherd Productions: *The Hanging Tree*
and *Love in a Goldfish Bowl*.

1960
Breakfast at Tiffany's, A Jurow-Shepherd
Production in New York.

1961
President, Charles Feldman Agency.

1962
Produced *The Pink Panther* in Rome, Italy,
and *Soldier in the Rain* in Los Angeles.

1963
Produced *The Great Race* at Warner Bros.

1964
Head of European production in London for
Warner Bros.

1968
Agent with Ashley-Steiner Agency in Los Angeles.

1970
Part of newly formed television department
at 20th Century Fox.

1971
Moved to Dallas, Texas.

1976
Reread the law and passed the Texas bar.

1977
Assistant District Attorney for Henry Wade
in Dallas.

1978
Formed Management West, a production
company.

1982–83
Produced *Waltz Across Texas* and co-produced
Terms of Endearment.

1984–85
Produced *Papa Was a Preacher*.

1986–1996
Distinguished visiting Professor at SMU teaching
"Business Opportunities in the Wide World of
Entertainment." KAAM Radio show *Martin
Jurow of Show Business*.

Introduction

∽

Martin Jurow's reputation preceded him. In movie jargon, it served as a trailer, a preview of coming attractions.

As a movie buff, I associated the name of Martin Jurow with indelible images—Audrey Hepburn perched on a fire escape, wistfully warbling "Moon River" in *Breakfast at Tiffany's*; Peter Sellers clumsily navigating the corridors of the Cortina d'Ampezzo resort in *The Pink Panther*; the custard pie fight to end all custard pie fights in *The Great Race*; Marlon Brando easing through town in a snakeskin jacket in *The Fugitive Kind*; Gary Cooper majestic on horseback riding through frontier horizons in *The Hanging Tree*.

These images reflected films of visual style and dramatic content. Initially I knew Martin Jurow simply as a movie producer who combined classic craftsmanship with mass audience appeal. Almost all his efforts were successes, and his few disappointments were never without honor.

Martin and his family moved to Dallas in 1971, when I was in my third year as entertainment writer for *The Dallas Morning News*. The gentleman I met was as elegant and articulate as you would expect the producer of *Breakfast at Tiffany's* and *The Pink Panther* to be. We encountered each other frequently at movie screenings and at Dallas's USA Film Festival, which he eagerly supported.

Martin was always willing to share his opinions, and we would exchange thoughts on various movies. The bond between movie lovers is at least as strong as the bond between sports fanatics who root for the same team. Frequently, professional barriers would disappear, and Martin and I became just a couple of movie buffs talking movies.

With each meeting, our friendship grew. I found Martin and his wife Erin-Jo to be keen observers of the human carnival. Having witnessed Tinseltown's most eccentric human behavior, they

Marty at Harvard Law School. He never smoked a pipe but loved using one as a prop.

harbor no illusions. But being decent people themselves, they emphasize and respond to the decency in others. Their family relationships are warm, loving, and respectful—an increasing rarity inside and outside the world of show business.

Through the years, virtually every celebrity who came to Dallas would call on Martin and Erin-Jo, making dinner with them a top priority. The entire scope of Martin's career became apparent by the people he knew. Not only was he a successful independent producer, he had also been head of the East Coast motion picture and theater departments at both MCA and the William Morris Agency. He was also an executive at Warner Bros. and with Hal Wallis at Paramount.

I quickly became aware of his diversity. He worked with major talents in film, stage, live performances, and television. He has been involved in the full spectrum of American entertainment and was on intimate terms with both its exhilaration and its heartache.

In collaborating on this look at his life, we worked together on Sunday afternoons for over five years. Each meeting brought delightful revelations. Martin had helped cast Frank Sinatra in *From Here to Eternity* and had been among the first to realize Elvis Presley's movie potential. He had even accompanied Lucille Ball and Desi Arnaz on their honeymoon.

Martin's life adventures began on Tompkins Avenue in Brooklyn, New York, where his family lived above the largest of the Jurows' millinery stores. Martin's mother Helena was a designer of ladies' hats. A natural artist, she created original designs, resplendent with feathers and ornaments. Large Manhattan stores often sent their own designers to look at her shops' display windows for fresh ideas. Martin's father Benjamin managed the stores, which employed more than a dozen women.

Although Helena Jurow was the prime mover in the business, she insisted that her shops bear her husband's name.

The Jurow home above the store consisted of seven well-appointed rooms, decorated in his mother's impeccable taste. Martin, his older brother Irving, and his younger sister Edna enjoyed a life of comfortable harmony.

Martin's earliest memories are of the symphony of street sounds and the aromas of neighborhood kitchens, delis, and bakeries. Merchants of all kinds—candy store, barber shop, dairy store, haberdashery—all mingled to create the rich tapestry of his daily life. His eyes still twinkle when he recalls the clanging of the Tompkins Avenue Trolley heading north to the Dodgers' Ebbets Field, where he spent summer days in the twenty-five-cent bleacher section. Even today, Martin says that, to him, the Dodgers mean Brooklyn.

One of the key neighborhood stores in Martin's memories is the optometrist shop, the site of his first personal encounter with a denizen of show business. Eddie Jackson—of the Clayton, Jackson and Durante musical comedy vaudeville team—often visited the optometrist shop next to the Jurows' main millinery shop. Eddie, a great talker, would book the threesome, and Martin would listen avidly as he made deals for himself, Lou Clayton and Jimmy Durante. Eddie, who possessed a persuasive singing and speaking voice, would sweet-talk agents into awarding the team higher salaries and better vaudeville halls, the Palace on Broadway being the apex of every vaudevillian's dreams. At that time, Martin was unaware of just how much show business savvy he was absorbing.

On most Saturdays, Martin and his friend Joey Ullman would visit neighbors' back yards, where Martin would perform a medley of his

Helena Jurow, 1902.

Benjamin Jurow, 1902.

favorite tunes: "I Wish I Could Shimmy Like My Sister Kate," "Tea for Two," "Give Me a June Night, the Moonlight, and You." As Martin sang, Joey would pick up the coins the neighbors would toss from their windows. Then they would head for the Classic, a plain neighborhood movie house with uncomfortable benchlike seats. Martin's earnings would pay for their nickel admissions. Mesmerized by the great Western serials, they mostly stood (oblivious to the uncomfortable seats) with their toy guns in their holsters, talking to

the screen—cheering the heroes and hissing the villains.

Martin discovered a cavalcade of talent on those Saturday afternoons. His Western heroes were William S. Hart, William Farnum, Dustin Farnum, and Tom Mix; the serial queens he admired were Pearl White and Ruth Roland. And he loved the comics, including Charlie Chaplin, Harold Lloyd, Buster Keaton, the demure Mary Pickford, and the swashbuckling Douglas Fairbanks. He was fascinated by such emerging stars as

Left to right, twelve-year-old Irving, five-year-old Marty, and one-year-old Edna Jurow, 1916. Happy hours in the family music room.

Ronald Colman, Myrna Loy, Clark Gable, Jean Harlow, and Greta Garbo. As they left the Classic each Saturday, Martin and Joey brandished their toy guns and pretended to be their celluloid heroes.

Martin remembers Sundays as the best day of the week: the family would dine at a fine restaurant, followed by a movie and a vaudeville act at Fox's Folly in downtown Brooklyn. Martin was enthralled by the assemblage of singers, dancers, acrobats, jugglers, and comics. He remembers especially the dancing comedian Pat Rooney, singer Harry Richman, and the formidable belter Sophie Tucker.

Then they would adjourn to Tomkins Avenue for a light supper and an evening in their small music room, listening to classical recordings on the Victrola—marveling at the vocal power of Enrico Caruso and Geraldine Farrar, and the technique and style of violinists Mischa Ellman and Jascha Heifetz. Martin's mother would stand beside the Victrola, explaining the operas' plots to the three Jurow children, who were spellbound by the intense musical dramas. Helena exchanged records with neighbors so that the Jurows had a circulating library of great recordings.

Both of his parents and his siblings encouraged Martin's interest in the arts. He never doubted that his life would in some way be involved in show business. He was a voracious reader and bought every newspaper he could find. Eddie Jackson gave him copies of *Weekly Variety*, which he would read cover to cover. He was determined to succeed, determined not just to make excellent grades but to retain what he learned. He says today that he has been able to apply virtually everything he learned in school later in his career. He has been blessed by powers of concentration and absorption. Consciously or unconsciously, he was always preparing for a life in the arts. However, he never took formal lessons in music, dance, acting, or any form of arts management. He simply absorbed everything he heard and saw.

Though Martin's was a comfortable childhood, two circumstances caused the Jurows to be circumspect about spending: a fraudulent friend convinced Benjamin he should invest in a resort hotel, in which the family ultimately lost a substantial amount of money; and the millinery business was changing. Custom hats with feathers, beads, and veils were going out of style, and department stores were opening their own "hat bars." Helena Jurow, suffering from heart trouble, closed her older shops and opened one in Manhattan at Broadway and 78th Street.

Both Martin and his brother Irving were among a group of academically talented young men of modest means who became protégés of James B. Munn, the scion of a wealthy insurance family and dean of the English department at Washington Square College, a branch of New York University on lower Fifth Avenue. In addition to paying for their college tuition, J. B., who would later become dean of Harvard's English department, would also pay for opera and symphony performances, as well as giving them charge accounts at impressive clothing stores. Dean Munn selected the group from a list of boys with good grades and deportment who had expressed an interest in Washington Square College. He felt

that all gifted young people should be exposed to the best things life had to offer.

Martin attended only one semester at Washington Square College, where his brother had preceded him. Although he loved the tempo of urban life, he wanted to explore other worlds and went to the library to learn about various small colleges in other settings. He was intrigued by John D. Rockefeller Jr.'s planned restoration of Williamsburg, Virginia. Dean Munn understood Martin's wish to leave New York and agreed for him to attend the College of William and Mary in Williamsburg. It was a small school with an enrollment of fifteen hundred students, mostly from the country's rural sections, and it appealed to Martin's desire for new horizons.

Martin decided to major in history with a minor in political science. By this time his brother Irving was practicing law and wanted eventually to bring Martin into his firm. He and Martin thought a history degree would provide a good stepping-stone to law school, and Martin was eager to learn more about his country's history. He figured that if his dreams of a career in show business did not work out, a law degree would be potentially useful. In those days, few colleges offered degrees in drama, but Martin knew that William and Mary had an active dramatics club, which he intended to join. He entered William and Mary in 1928, determined to excel in both history and extracurricular activities for his brother's sake as well as J. B. Munn's.

At William and Mary, Martin supplemented Munn's contributions by various entrepreneurial ventures: he engaged two African-Americans, deacons of their church, to help deliver laundry to students. The three of them rode through Williamsburg's picturesque streets in a horse and buggy; Martin proudly earned the munificent sum of seventy-five dollars per semester. Martin remembers what a harsh time this was for African-Americans in the South; he befriended his two workers, buying them clothing and visiting their homes in times of illness.

Martin was leader of a little band, the William and Mary Indians, and following the example of bandleader Rudy Vallee, used a megaphone. This was before the introduction of easily adaptable microphones, and Martin would circle the venue where they were playing, singing into the megaphone. The ten-member band would play for campus events every other week. As they played, the audience would dance the Shag, and band members would alternate joining them. Admission to a dance was fifty cents. Covering all bases,

Martin also had the Coca-Cola concession and eventually found that he could even send money home.

Martin recalls that his most valuable experiences at William and Mary were in the theater classes of multitalented drama coach Althea Hunt. A woman of passion and conviction, Ms. Hunt had a great instinct for spotting young talent. As he looks back, he realizes how much of his own enthusiasm for discovering talent he absorbed watching her. Under Althea's direction Martin starred in student productions as Sir Toby in *Twelfth Night*, Shylock in *The Merchant of Venice*, and the young Eugene O'Neill in *Ah, Wilderness!*.

His favorite role—one he almost didn't get— was in *Berkeley Square*, the ethereal romantic fan-

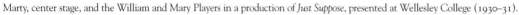

Marty, center stage, and the William and Mary Players in a production of *Just Suppose*, presented at Wellesley College (1930–31).

Tennis anyone? Marty at William and Mary College, 1928.

tasy that would be filmed with Leslie Howard in 1933. (Martin played a modern man who travels back in time to nineteenth-century London, thus fulfilling onstage his burning desire to see more of the world.) The show's original star, Piggy Diggs, a strapping six-footer, ran away to join the newly formed air force just before the show was to open. Martin was then tapped to be the star, but Piggy's costumes had to be altered to fit Martin's five-foot-six-inch frame. Thanks to a team of seamstresses who worked all night, the show did go on.

Martin belonged to a small movie club in Williamsburg; club members got a discount because they bought meal tickets from the movie house's owner. Saturday nights Martin would enjoy films starring actors such as Greta Garbo, the Marx Brothers, and Charlie Chaplin. He could easily spot emerging talent like Joan Crawford, with whom he would later work at Warner Bros., and Gary Cooper, who would star in Martin's first personal production in 1958.

Though Saturday nights at the movies were wonderful, Wednesday nights at Williamsburg would leave a lasting impression on the young man. As Martin was becoming acquainted with the colonial village, he had noticed faces full of curiosity and emotion staring out at him from a grim-looking building then uncharitably known as the insane asylum. He recruited a small group of friends to go with him to the asylum each Wednesday evening; they brought records to play on a Victrola and asked the inmates to dance. The inmates were pleased at the attention, and when Martin and his friends would change partners and cut in on them, their faces would light up. From being downcast and feeling isolated, the inmates—for those Wednesday evenings at least—would beam with pride and renewed self-esteem. Martin learned a valuable lesson: making people feel

important could reap manifold emotional and practical dividends.

Sometimes Martin would sit with Mr. and Mrs. John D. Rockefeller Jr. on the front porch of their Williamsburg home. He found them to be a quiet, pleasant couple, interested in all aspects of life in the village they were restoring. Mr. Rockefeller instilled in him the importance of financial stability, of having sufficient resources for your own needs and for helping others. Rockefeller's advice that you should always have something to fall back on was an additional spur to Martin's pursuit of a law degree after graduating from William and Mary.

During his college days, Martin held various jobs at summer camps. He spent the summer of 1929 as head counselor at the Charles Atlas Camp in upstate New York, run by the great muscle-builder himself with some one hundred children in attendance. Martin discovered that though Atlas might be muscular, he was also lazy. Just getting him to reach a standing position each morning was torturous work requiring three very hefty campers, recruited the previous night. Martin would then carefully explain to him that it was time to greet the children and lead them in their morning calisthenics. Once fully awake, Charles Atlas was always courteous and on Friday evenings would treat everyone to the spectacle of watching him tear apart the New York telephone directory.

The adult camps in the Adirondacks, where Martin worked in the summer of 1933, allowed him some creative freedom. As social director and singing waiter, he would perform his own songs, winning applause with lyrics like "I'm gonna knock on the door / peek in / lift the latch / and walk into / my mammy's arms."

He suspected, though, that he was not another Al Jolson. And he also realized that he was not another Clark Gable or Gary Cooper. His short physical stature—in the days before Michael J. Fox, Dustin Hoffman, and Tom Cruise—made him decide, reluctantly, that he should give up any thoughts of acting and pursue law and arts management.

In 1932, with his history degree from Williamsburg in hand, Martin told J. B. Munn that he wanted to go on to law school. Martin asked his patron if he'd help him if he was accepted into Harvard Law School. Dean Munn said yes, and in 1935, after three strenuous academic years at that august institution, Martin Jurow received his law degree.

Upon his graduation, he was determined to find a job that would combine his love of the law with his love of the entertainment world. He set his sights on one law firm, that of New York's foremost entertainment lawyer, Nathan Burkan, whose name he saw frequently in the pages of *Weekly Variety*. From his insatiable reading of the *New York Times*, Martin knew of Burkan's involvement in high profile cases; Burkan was a political leader and a Tammany Hall hero whose roster of clients included Al Jolson, Charlie Chaplin, Mae West, Jimmy Durante, Eddie Cantor, and George M. Cohan.

Martin carefully composed a fan letter to Nathan Burkan, mentioning Burkan's political successes and show business triumphs. He even commented on the attorney's recent marriage and his appendectomy. Martin wrote that he'd be in touch when he came to New York to take the state bar exam. When Martin got to New York, he immediately went to see Mr. Burkan's chief telephone operator and asked her to let him know when Burkan won any kind of victory. Finally, two weeks later, she called with the news that Burkan had won a major victory in the custody battle over "Little Gloria" Vanderbilt.

Marty, lower left, with fellow members of Harvard University's Pollock Law Club.

Within seconds of receiving that call, Martin picked up the telephone to offer his congratulations to Burkan, who invited him to his office. On the spot, Burkan offered the eager young Harvard graduate a job as his assistant at twenty-six dollars a week. Despite the meager salary, Martin didn't have to be asked twice. Turning down offers from out-of-town law firms for two or three times what Burkan proposed to pay, Martin had answered the siren's call of show business.

Some of Martin's assistant-to-Burkan duties were less than glamorous. Every morning at Burkan's apartment, it was Martin's responsibility to test the shower to make sure it was the exact temperature Burkan had specified. And Martin also was required to pour a pitcher of ice water into Burkan's hands so he could rinse his eyes after he'd doused them with warm water. All these unglamorous chores stood him in good stead in later years when Martin would need to soothe the ruffled feathers of a star by tending to some personal matter unrelated to the project at hand, like getting a longer extension cord for Natalie Wood or flying in Jackie Gleason's favorite hair stylist or Shirley MacLaine's favorite manicurist.

Martin's other duties at Burkan's firm were more substantive. Burkan asked Martin to write the brief when ASCAP, the revered American Society of Composers, Authors, and Publishers, came under siege by the Department of Justice. Using the phrase "control the music over the world," the Justice Department claimed that ASCAP had a monopoly on music.

With the great author/composer/performer George M. Cohan, Martin went to Washington and showered the attorney general's office with such classical names as Brahms, Schubert, Schumann, Verdi, Puccini, Chopin, Mozart, Beethoven, and Liszt. Since the Department of Justice had not specified "modern music" in citing ASCAP's alleged attempts at monopoly, Martin took advantage of that lethal legal loophole, stating that every classical composer from Bach to Rimsky-Korsakov had survived without even a nod from ASCAP. Martin helped the Burkan office win the case and defeat the government.

During his time at the Burkan law firm, Martin would attend the theater every evening before he returned to his West End Avenue apartment. He couldn't afford many dates but enjoyed having an expense account (a perk that made his low salary palatable). He saw Alfred Lunt and Lynn Fontanne in *Idiot's Delight* and Tallulah

Bankhead in *The Little Foxes*. He went to musicals, the Scandals, the Vanities, the Revues. Occasionally, he'd see movies, though at this point in his early career, he preferred to study theater.

He turned down job offers from leading members of the Mob, powerful men who invested in Broadway shows, restaurants, and nightclubs as well as specific entertainers like Texas Guinan and Joe E. Lewis. They wanted a clean representative for transactions. However, Martin had no desire to join their syndicate and declined—with no hard feelings.

Elated with the ASCAP victory, Martin was even more exhilarated about meeting the celebrities who populated the Burkan law offices. These first-hand meetings whetted Martin's appetite for more contact with stars. Here he first witnessed the eccentricities, foibles, vanities, insecurities and the survival instincts of stars like Mae West, Al Jolson, and Eddie Cantor.

Martin realized that when Mae West and Nathan Burkan were together in a room, there was a meeting of two masters: he knew the law, and she knew show business. Martin saw that she had an uncanny knack for measuring phoniness, perhaps because she herself was a priestess of pretention. She arrived in a white limo, all dressed in white, accompanied by musclemen dressed in white, and demanded that her rooms, drapes and even entire hotel suites had to be decorated entirely in white. Martin realized that he had a great seat at an exciting performance. Years later, when Martin was with the William Morris Agency in the 1950s, he would represent Mae West and consider her a good friend.

Burkan's clients included legendary singing dynamos Al Jolson and Eddie Cantor. Martin remembers them as full of bombast. And full of ego. Later he would work with movie stars ranging from Errol Flynn to Marlon Brando, from Bette Davis to Shirley MacLaine, from Humphrey Bogart to Jack Nicholson. They all had egos of various sizes. But none had an ego as gigantic as Cantor's or Jolson's.

Almost all the film celebrities had been under contract at one time. They knew what it was like to be answerable to someone. But Cantor and Jolson created themselves as show people, and their sense of divinity was great.

The banjo-eyed Cantor loved wearing his full-length raccoon coat in all kinds of weather, and he somehow managed to make his eyes even wider whenever he was photographed in it. Martin realized that Cantor was studying him during visits to the Burkan offices, sizing up his actions and nodding with what seemed like approval. One day Cantor broke some startling news: he wanted Martin as a son-in-law.

He wasn't terribly clear about which of his five daughters he wanted Martin to marry. But he said he felt Martin would make a good son-in-law for him. Martin didn't know what to do. He did not want to marry any of the daughters, and one thing he was absolutely certain of: he did not want Eddie Cantor for a father-in-law.

So he appealed to Cantor's ego, telling him that he was simply an assistant who had willingly accepted a twenty-six-dollar-a-week salary. He pleaded that he was not worthy of being married to Cantor's daughter, that he was not worthy of being his son-in-law. Such a display of deference caught Eddie's attention. Cantor tossed it back and forth in his mind. He reflected upon it. He thanked Martin for his honesty and never spoke of it again. As Martin recalls, a dowry was never mentioned.

Of the Burkan roster, George M. Cohan, America's Yankee Doodle Dandy, had the most profound influence on Martin. He saw that George

M. Cohan never stopped learning, never thought of himself as being too old and experienced to try something new. He was always dapper, elegant, and debonair. Martin still remembers Cohan's custom-made shirts, narrow ties, and the narrow lapels on his suits. Cohan wore hand-made shoes, and Martin was fascinated by them, determined at some point that he would have some, too. Cohan was the first person Martin considered a total champion.

But Martin's days of having hand-made shoes like George M. Cohan's were still some years in the future. He was devastated when Burkan died unexpectedly of a heart attack; he knew the firm would not be the same without him. Martin wrote another letter, this time to George Abbott.

As he had with Burkan, he praised Abbott for all that he had done and was doing. (George Abbott would die in 1995 at the age of 107, a legendary force behind classic productions from the 1930s through the 1960s: *Damn Yankees*, *The Pajama Game*, *Room Service*, *The Boys from Syracuse*, *Three Men on a Horse*, *Brother Rat*, *Boy Meets Girl*.)

Abbott was known for a great sense of comic timing, and all his shows were laced with peppy dialogue and constant action. Despite this, Martin remembers him as a man of few words who was always called "Mr. Abbott."

At their first meeting, Martin told Abbott that he wanted to be assistant company manager. The producer said there was no such position. But they struck a deal. Abbott would create the position of assistant company manager if Martin would understudy six roles in *Boy Meets Girl*. So at the age of twenty-seven, Martin became the youngest company manager touring the country, at the salary of forty dollars a-week.

One of the stage managers for *Boy Meets Girl*

was a young fellow named Harold Prince, who called Martin "coach." In the 1950s, Hal Prince would become one of the greatest Broadway directors of musicals. At that time, Martin recognized that he was incredibly focused, always managing to accomplish whatever he set out to do. Martin recalls that Prince was knowledgeable about theater and attended every show he didn't have to pay for.

Martin's relationship with Abbott reached a turning point when the producer wanted to send him out on the road in a lead role in the military comedy *Brother Rat*.

Sixty years later Martin remembers their conversation verbatim.

"How tall are you?" Martin asked Abbott.

"I'm six-foot-three. Why do you ask?"

"Because I'm five-foot-six. I cannot compete with gifted people your size. I am not a leading man. Clark Gable is tall. Gary Cooper is tall. Joel McCrea is tall. I am not."

Abbott had no more plays to tour, and after three years, Martin felt he had learned as much as he could under his tutelage. He sought a new situation, where he could put his legal background to use, and he decided to look for a job in an agency, where his goal would be the representation of talent.

In 1940, as he had before, he wrote a letter. This time it was to Dr. Jules Stein, the omnipotent president of the Music Corporation of America, the giant entertainment conglomerate known as MCA. Martin felt this could be the turning point of his life, a direct route to what had become his ultimate goal of producing his own films.

Dr. Stein and his top associate Lew Wasserman, who, upon Dr. Stein's death, inherited his title of MCA president, were intent on representing talent in every area. Their plans for MCA consisted of an expansion so enormous that acerbic critics referred to the company as "The Octopus." Their arms would reach across the entire entertainment field. They even bought the Ice Capades. They not only represented the era's golden bandleaders—Goodman, Lombardo, Xavier Cugat, Tommy and Jimmy Dorsey, Harry James, and Kay Kyser—they expanded to artists of every calling—actors, writers, producers. When they wanted Danny Kaye, they simply bought Columbia Artists Agency, which owned his contract.

When attending any important meeting that concerned his future, Martin started a practice of parking at least a block away from the designated building and giving himself a pep talk as he walked. By the time he entered the building, any apprehension had evaporated. This technique worked for Martin all through his career and never more effectively than on the day he met Dr. Jules Stein of MCA. They enjoyed an instant rapport. Before long, Martin was head of MCA's East Coast motion picture and legitimate theater divisions and involved in every other area of entertainment. And his salary was no longer forty dollars a week, but ten times that amount, together with an insurance policy for twenty-five thousand dollars.

George Abbott was a client, and MCA represented him in the movie sale of *Too Many Girls* with Eddie Bracken, Desi Arnaz, Van Johnson, and the sensual singer Diosa Costello. At MCA, Martin also worked with Eddie Albert and June Allyson.

Martin remembers Van Johnson as an extremely attractive young man, an object of desire in the eyes of both genders. One night after *Too Many Girls*, he could tell that some of the chorus boys were beckoning Van upstairs to their dressing rooms. He knew major companies, including

When Marty was at MCA, he watched as Gene Kelly strutted to the stage to audition and knew he would be a star. They never worked together but remained friends through the years.

Metro-Goldwyn-Mayer, were interested in signing the appealing young actor. In those days, private lives were carefully guarded—movie moguls might be afraid that Van's upstairs activities would pose problems.

Martin walked over to the voluptuous Diosa Costello and said simply, "Could you detain Van?"

No other words were necessary. Her eyes sparkled and her smile beamed. "Of course I will, Marty. I will be happy to detain Van."

And detain him she did. She ushered Van into her dressing room, for what Martin is certain was a memorable evening.

The next time he saw Diosa, the glint in her eye was unmistakable. "Anytime you need me, Marty. Anytime at all."

While he was with MCA, Martin was proud to represent George M. Cohan in his final theatrical appearance, in a 1941 play called *The Return of the Vagabond*. As the show neared the end of its run, they sat together and reminisced. The show biz veteran looked at Martin in gentle appraisal and said simply, "It's been a grand old time, hasn't it, Marty?"

"It's been a grand old time," Martin replied. "And you're a grand trouper."

Martin always had pride but tried not to be prideful. Early in his career as an MCA agent, the Shubert brothers would give him tickets on the last row of their theaters. As Martin became more influential, the tickets improved—mid-theater, center. But he told them he preferred the back row, not wishing to acknowledge that they gave him better seats only after his status increased.

Ever acquisitive, MCA bought Columbia Artists' full group of players, one of whom, Erin-Jo Guinn, would become Martin's wife.

Erin-Jo played ingenue parts on daytime radio serials and toured New England in summer stock and winter stock, portraying Emily in *Our Town* and Alice in *You Can't Take It With You*. Martin often noticed her in their offices, and when she did a screen test for Paramount, he watched it with her and her mother. Erin-Jo thought she had made a terrible test and wept on Martin's shoulder. That night he told his mother that he had found the girl of his dreams.

But he first needed to get his personal life in perfect order. He had been dating the young actress Rosemary Lane, who with siblings Priscilla and Lola formed the thespic threesome known as the Lane Sisters. Martin enjoyed spending time with Rosemary but knew that marriage was not in their future. Typical of his sense of personal honor, he wanted to bring their relationship to a closure before pursuing Erin-Jo.

Four months later, in February of 1942, he asked Erin-Jo to join him at a revival of *Porgy and Bess*. Afterwards, they went to a nightclub on 57th Street and saw a new comic named Danny Thomas. They stayed until two A.M. and had a wonderful time. The next night they went to a steakhouse and then to see *Banjo Eyes* starring Eddie Cantor, who not so long ago had wanted to be Martin's father-in-law.

At the restaurant, Martin did something that Erin-Jo said convinced her he was the man for her. As a Texas-born beefeater, she couldn't decide between a steak or roast beef. He told the waiter to bring both.

They were married six weeks later, on April 18, 1942, in the Christopher Wren Chapel of Martin's alma mater, the College of William and Mary. Althea Hunt's drama class added a festive theatrical touch, attending in costume for their rehearsal of *Hedda Gabler*.

Erin-Jo Gwynne (née Guinn), 1941, photographed by celebrity photographer Murray Korman in New York. When he met her, Marty told his mother he'd found the girl of his dreams.

At MCA Martin also worked with Robert E. Sherwood, whose plays included *The Petrified Forest*, which made Humphrey Bogart a Broadway star, and *Idiot's Delight* and *There Shall Be No Night*, both of which starred Alfred Lunt and Lynn Fontanne. Martin sent both Van Johnson and June Allyson to Hollywood, where they became bobbysoxers' favorites and top moneymakers at Metro-Goldwyn-Mayer.

Another actress whom he sent to Hollywood was Ava Gardner. He always kept in touch with important modeling agencies, and Ava was modeling for the powerful Harry Conover Agency.

Martin remembers the youthful Ava vividly.

"She was gorgeous and sexual. All she had to do was enter the El Morocco nightclub, and every pair of eyes followed her across the room. She knew she was voluptuous, and she had the confidence of a woman who realizes that she possesses what men covet."

He represented the ultimate GI pin-up Betty Grable and Eve Arden, later television's immortal Our Miss Brooks. He worked with Ray Bolger and the ever-bombastic Al Jolson. He represented Ethel Merman in *Panama Hattie*, Gertrude Lawrence in *Lady in the Dark*, and Eddie Albert in *The Boys from Syracuse*.

He also worked with the African-American dancer Katharine Dunham, who had her own troupe specializing in Jamaican dance. She completely captivated Al Jolson. But Martin wryly recalls that she lived in a West Side brownstone five floors up, which were at least two too many for Joley to manage.

During those years came the introduction of television. Martin witnessed its beginning at the 1939 World's Fair. The response was phenomenal,

The great comic Eddie Bracken and his wife Connie, leaving on their honeymoon in 1938. Eddie, Connie, Marty, and Erin-Jo remained great friends through the years.

Marty and Erin-Jo, photographed by Phil Silvers at B-Bar-H guest ranch near Palm Springs, December, 1948. That explains the big grins.

and Martin knew it would provide a great learning experience. Television proved to be a training ground for writers, directors, actors, and producers, whose ranks he hoped to join.

In the early days of television, talented newcomers were thrilled at the prospect of flexing their artistic muscles in the new medium. Actors with names like James Dean, Grace Kelly, and Paul Newman made their first impressions under the direction of fresh young talents like John Frankenheimer, George Roy Hill, and Arthur Penn. The television plays were written by the likes of Paddy Chayefsky, Reginald Rose, Rod Serling, and Tad Mosel.

Martin was happy at MCA but knew he would never be at peace with himself until he carried the mantle of production. He admits he sometimes ponders the wisdom of leaving MCA, but he has no

regrets. When the movie industry beckoned, he headed west to the Gold Coast. His Hollywood experiences surpassed even his wildest expectations.

In our Sunday afternoon reveries, each meeting brought a new anecdote, a fresh memory, a delicate yet delicious insight into a famous personality.

Martin Jurow's cavalcade of memories represents more than half a century of American show business and popular American culture. Some of the anecdotes poignantly depict the insecurities of celebrityhood. Others hilariously target star-sized egos. All reflect the compassion of a man who has led a long and loving life, without regret or rancor. It's a banquet of celebrated names and faces, remembered with disarming honesty.

And now, in Martin's voice, let the stories begin.

PHILIP WUNTCH
Dallas, Texas
March 2001

Marty Jurow Seein' Stars

1

Warner Time

~

"What do you think, J. L.?," I asked, summoning what I hoped was sufficient diplomacy. "Do you think you should go outside and welcome Joan Crawford to the studio? Maybe even escort her to the wardrobe department?"

I was in the office of Jack L. Warner, head of Warner Bros. Studio, and I had just noticed Joan Crawford arriving on the lot to test for the title role in *Mildred Pierce.*

J. L.'s answer was typical J. L. Warner.

"That has-been! Why waste my time? We're only using her because Stanwyck's too busy! I've got better things to do than say hello to that dame."

What I had seen was not the imperious Queen Joan who had glittered as a 1930s screen icon at Metro-Goldwyn-Mayer. Instead, this was a weary working woman who clutched her handbag to her chest and walked with her shoulders slumped, her eyes fixed on the sidewalk.

Warner Bros. was preparing an adaptation of James Cain's *Mildred Pierce*, and the brass reluctantly considered asking Joan Crawford to test for the part of hard-boiled, soft-hearted Mildred. The indomitable Ms. Crawford had fallen on hard times. A series of flops prompted MGM not to renew her contract, and she had not made a film in two years. Warner Bros. executives entertained the notion of casting her only after their contract actresses could not fit it in their schedules.

Joan's placement within the Hollywood hierarchy had always been her primary concern. All of Hollywood knew that her decade-long affair with Clark Gable had ended in the late 1930s when he became a bigger star than she. Her sense of insecurity demanded that she be a bigger star than the man in her life, and in turn he would be beholden to her. At MGM, writers had been assigned to create vehicles specifically for her. And here she was, reduced to testing for a film that Bette Davis,

At left, boss J. L. Warner, at his most jovial, with Marty.

Barbara Stanwyck, Ann Sheridan and Ida Lupino didn't have time for.

I knew that with the martyred Joan, timing was of the essence. I ran to greet her. I told her how thrilled everyone at Warner Bros. was to have her at the studio. I explained in detail that the studio had wanted her for years but MGM refused to loan her out.

As I talked, a striking transformation took place. Her posture turned regal. Her eyes glowed. Her smile combined simple gratitude with queenly noblesse oblige. Yes, she was indeed thrilled to be at Warner Bros. Yes, she couldn't wait to do the test. And she hoped to do justice to a part as rich and rewarding as Mildred Pierce. Oh, and thank you so much for the personal greeting.

In a matter of mere moments, Joan Crawford Unemployed Actress became Joan Crawford Movie Star. Her performance in *Mildred Pierce* won an Academy Award and recharged her career.

J. L.'s cantankerous attitude had compelled me to employ the lesson I learned while I was in college at Willliam and Mary, when each week I led a group of students to meet with the inmates at a mental hospital in Williamsburg. We played records and asked them to dance with us, making each of them feel important. Like those inmates who couldn't wait to dance to the Victrola on Wednesday nights, even Joan Crawford needed to feel sought-after.

I learned early in my Warner Bros. tenure never to be surprised at anything Jack L. Warner might say. I had been at the studio only a week when J. L.'s secretary informed me that I was to watch dailies with him. (Dailies are scenes shot the previous day and an important barometer of a picture's progress.) Feeling proud to be asked, I joined him in the screening room, and we started watching the scenes. Suddenly he stood up and halted the screening.

"What are you doing?" he glared as he pointed his ever-present cigar in my direction.

I was surprised at the question but knew better than to make him ask twice.

"Why, I'm sharpening pencils," I replied, as casually as I could.

"And why are you sharpening pencils?" he demanded, as if using the pencil sharpener in his studio's screening room constituted an act of treason.

"So I can take notes, so I can learn from you," I said, again striving for casual dignity.

He twirled his cigar and retorted, "I want no notes, no written word to leave this screening room. Get rid of the pencil and the pad! And don't ever use the pencil sharpener in this room again!"

I learned early that in Hollywood the most ordinary act can be met with an extraordinary response.

I came to California in 1943 as first assistant to Jack Warner, the ruling sibling of the Warner Bros. Studio. Working for Warner was baptism by fire. But the flames were always colorful and sometimes even beautiful.

In New York, I had worked as East Coast talent chief for Warner Bros. Every day I played gin rummy at lunch with Harry, Sam, and Albert, all of whom were Warner brothers, although more jocular than that most daunting of siblings, the Warner brother named Jack. We enjoyed each other's bonhomie, and they were dutifully impressed by my Harvard Law School credentials. They thought I would go far in the business and recommended me to Jack.

From the vantage point of today's Hollywood, it's difficult to grasp the absolute power that the movie moguls had during the 1930s and 1940s. They were pashas, emperors, and sovereigns. They favored an appearance of moral rectitude but sometimes behaved like pagan Bacchanalians. Like the

Roman Emperors of old, they commanded both gladiators and slave girls, which, when translated to Hollywood terms, meant studio employees and contract players. But whatever can be said about their follies, all of them shared one virtue: they were passionate about movies.

Jack L. Warner reigned over a supreme kingdom that appropriately included some of Hollywood's toughest stars: Humphrey Bogart, Bette Davis, James Cagney, Errol Flynn, Edward G. Robinson, Olivia de Havilland, Ida Lupino, Lauren Bacall, John Garfield, and Ronald Reagan.

Aside from Warners' stable of stars, with its tough guys and sometimes even tougher dames, there was an extraordinary stock company consisting of character actors Peter Lorre, Claude Rains, Sydney Greenstreet, Frank McHugh, Pat O'Brien, Victor Franzon, Guy Kibbee and S. K. "Cuddles" Sakall. Crew members were also under contract.

It was one big family. Maybe not one big *happy* family. But professionally, it functioned perfectly, supplying moviegoers with hours of enchantment. If, like some families, it was dysfunctional on an emotional level, at least it was dysfunctional in colorful ways.

J. L. was a dictator who never doubted his own judgment. And he was a man of mercurial moods. In 1941, longtime Warners producer Jesse Lasky, having just shepherded the blockbuster *Sergeant York* and having been told by J. L. that he would always have a home at Warners, received a telegram from J. L. demanding his termination. After a smash like *Sergeant York*, Lasky's services were getting more expensive, and J. L. liked to cut corners. But studio insiders felt he was making a statement: J. L. wanted to appear to be the man behind *Sergeant York*, and he couldn't assume that role as long as Jesse Lasky was at the same studio.

Yet when I look back, I am awestruck by the cavalcade of important movies made while I was there:

Classics like *Casablanca* and *The Maltese Falcon*, adventures like *Action in the North Atlantic*, *High Sierra*, and *Captains of the Clouds*, romantic dramas like *Now, Voyager* and *The Constant Nymph*, patriotic musicals like *This Is the Army* and *Thank Your Lucky Stars*. All were made under the personal supervision of the studio's head of production, Hal B. Wallis, who would play an important part in my future.

At Warners I got to know virtually everyone under contract. Humphrey Bogart liked to surround himself with men who enhanced his own illusion of toughness. Around the studio, he preened when seen with tough, ominous men who lent him the desired sinister air. He would talk tough and walk tough when he was with them. But when they were nowhere to be seen, Bogart was merely a schoolyard prankster.

After I had been at Warners for a short while, Bogey started a rumor that I was a spy for Jack L. Warner. When I made my morning rounds of the soundstages, I noticed a chilly silence on the sets.

And then, away from the soundstages, I came upon an unforgettable scene. Bette Davis was upbraiding Bogart in very unladylike language. She had learned of his rumor-mongering and rushed to my defense. Bette knew the inner workings of the studio as thoroughly as any executive, and she knew I was not a spy for J. L.

It was a spectacular sight: Bette raging, Bogart cowering. As Hurricane Bette continued her assault, Bogey nervously tried to light and relight a cigarette. Bette Davis definitely was someone you would want on your side in time of combat.

J. L., as Jack was usually called, dreaded all meetings with his stars, but he was interested in knowing what they wanted, whether he planned to accommodate or ignore their requests. He was afraid of Bette, terrified of what she might do if provoked. With my office next to his, he instructed me to keep my door open so I could see if a star was striding ominously toward his office. That was the extent of my studio espionage.

Later Bogart apologized for his mischief. Or at least he apologized as much as Humphrey Bogart could. He went to Bette and said, "I told Martin I was sorry, and I really am sorry." He never said a word to me.

He mellowed somewhat after marrying Lauren Bacall, but apologies were never his forte.

Steve Trilling was Jack Warner's executive assistant. Poor man! J. L. treated him shamefully, working him without mercy and without a single word of praise or gratitude. Everyone brought their complaints to Steve, with gripes ranging from the location of their dressing rooms to their desire for more publicity. When Steve relayed them to J. L., the bombastic studio chief was always ready to shoot the messenger.

Steve was protective of his position. My office had one less window than his, and my name on the office door was in smaller lettering than his. When I saw how burdened he was, I felt he was entitled.

Not that I enjoyed anything resembling free time. But the work was fascinating. My duties were expansive. Early in the morning, I would visit each set and check on the comfort of the stars. That duty alone could be quite a feat. Quickly I learned that every star's dressing room was to be lavishly decorated, with meals delivered to the dressing room door. Most wanted drivers to and from the studio. The more artistic and/or ambitious sought to give their opinions of directors and screenwriters and wanted the right to watch dailies.

I would meet with producers and directors like William Dieterle (1939's *Juarez*), Michael Curtiz (1943's *Casablanca*), Raoul Walsh (1949's *White Heat*), Vincent Sherman (1942's *The Hard*

Way), Edmund Goulding (1939's *The Old Maid*), Delmer Daves (1943's *Destination Tokyo*) and Curtis Bernhardt (1947's *Possessed*). And I was always available to Mr. Wallis.

The studio's screenwriters were housed in a separate building. Writers generally create at their own pace, but at Warners they had to punch a timeclock. Sometimes when I walked past the writers' building, I would see twin brothers, screenwriters and college boxing champions Julius J. Epstein and Philip G. Epstein pounding at the bars that enclosed the building's window, comically pleading, "Let us out! Let us out!" But the Epsteins stayed at Warners and wrote the screenplay for *Casablanca*.

I supervised the casting of all Warner Bros. pictures and each week read the fresh pages of Warner writers. I also read all the scripts of my colleagues and inspected new novels and stageplays to see if they were movie material. Among my recommendations were *Mr. Skeffington*, which became one of Bette Davis's last big hits for the studio, and *Destination Tokyo*, which provided Cary Grant with one of his most memorable noncomedic roles.

I was also fascinated by new, improved equipment for sound and cameras. I would often spend time with film editors. After the final shot, the directors frequently were off to their next project. I would help supervise the editing, offering advice and learning much from the editing staff. When I later produced my own pictures, all this experience would prove invaluable.

Saturdays were for production meetings, with special emphasis on budgetary matters. I would walk to lunch with J. L. and watch dailies with him. He was a ruthless businessman and a practical joker who loved having the last laugh. He enjoyed keeping everyone on their toes, making certain they were never sure where they stood with him. He tried to keep major stars in line by casting actors with similar personalities as threats. Ida Lupino was Bette Davis's threat; Dane Clark was John Garfield's.

Frequently, at the end of the day, J. L. would come to me and say, "Let's turn out the lights." During those brief moments, he was more pleasant. He had weathered another day, and he would happily twirl his cigar.

I would attend previews of every movie and often my wife Erin-Jo and I would be invited to his home to watch screenings of other studios' product. At previews, J. L. would act like a vaudevillian jokester. But after each preview, he would be very serious in asking the opinion of his masseur Abdul the Turk, who limited his critical evaluation to "good" and "not-so-good."

I would also play tennis at J. L.'s house, only to have him nudge me off the court, quipping "Get out of here, Mickey Rooney!" He would then continue my game.

It was also my job to tell a young actor named Ronald Reagan that he would not star in an upcoming feature called *Everybody Comes to Rick's*, which had been scheduled for him, Ann Sheridan and Dennis Morgan. Ronnie, as everyone called him, was disappointed but not rancorous.

Everybody Comes to Rick's became the classic *Casablanca*. As Ronnie's political career progressed, it became fashionable to embellish the story, saying he had lost the colorful role of cynical Rick, immortalized by Humphrey Bogart. But Reagan was never meant to be Rick. The role he lost was that of Victor Laszlo, the Resistance leader married to Rick's former love, Ilsa. Dennis Morgan and Ann Sheridan were originally scheduled to be Rick and Ilsa.

Years later, Erin-Jo and I would smile at one of our Reagan memories. We were on our honeymoon in San Francisco when we ran into Ronnie and his then-wife, Jane Wyman. We had dinner

together. Ronnie was sweet and relaxed. Jane, on the other hand, was a powerhouse personality, a tough cookie with a flamboyantly profane vocabulary that Ronnie seemed to enjoy.

And why the casting change for *Casablanca?* The answer is pure Hollywood. Those prankster Epstein twins, Julius and Philip, went to a party and fell in love with a woman they met at the Hollywood gathering, a young actress named Ingrid Bergman. Ingrid had been well-received in her Hollywood debut picture *Intermezzo* and in *Dr. Jekyll and Mr. Hyde* with Spencer Tracy, but she was not yet a major star.

The Epsteins restructured the script completely, changing the American heroine to a woman of foreign birth. They convinced Hal Wallis that this would give the romantic situation more depth. Out were Reagan, Sheridan, and Morgan, all of whom were A-minus, rather than A, stars. In were Bogart, Bergman, and Paul Henreid. And Michael Curtiz, one of the studio's top craftsmen, was to direct. And so a classic was born because the Epstein brothers, like so many men in Hollywood, were bewitched by Ingrid Bergman.

Another actor with whom I worked closely at Warners was Little Caesar himself, Edward G. Robinson. Snarling, scowling and sneering on-screen, he was even stranger away from the camera. He could be remarkably passive, considering his screen image. But he always insisted on being treated as a top star, perhaps overcompensating for his lack of traditional movie-star handsomeness.

There were two sides to the off-screen Eddie. One was the roaring gangster; Eddie never wanted anyone to doubt that he could turn into a gangland Caesar if things did not go his way. He also took delight in being known as an art lover, and he and his wife Gladys acquired the most renowned collection of Impressionist paintings in California. Some Hollywood collectors were taken advantage of by con artists, but Eddie and Gladys knew their art.

I knew Eddie for years after I left Warners. He was a naturally suspicious person, and at times it was impossible to imagine him at peace with the world. He was not blacklisted during the shameful McCarthy Era, but his political loyalties were suspect. This resulted in his being offered less work. His only son was in constant trouble with the law and made several suicide attempts. And, finally, Gladys and he were divorced after twenty-nine years of marriage. Gladys took most of his art treasures. Eddie sat alone in his house, staring at the blank walls and almost going insane. He became a total recluse.

During the early 1950s, when I was working for the William Morris Agency in New York, a play by the gifted Paddy Chayefsky was making the rounds. It was called *Middle of the Night*, and I knew that the lead role would be perfect for Eddie. The play was about a middle-aged man's relationship with a young woman. I knew that Eddie's own tastes for female companionship never subsided, even during his saddest periods.

He had instructed his housekeeper not to let any visitors invade his solitary confinement. But she knew Eddie and I were friendly and allowed me to enter the dark room where he sat alone. Script in hand, I was determined that he do the Chayefsky play and find solace on Broadway rather than Hollywood.

I opened the drapes and said in a soft voice, "I want you to read this play, Eddie. I'm taking you back to Broadway."

A multitude of emotions clouded Eddie's tough-guy face. He was defiant because his privacy had been disturbed. But he was delighted that someone actually wanted him for an important acting job.

Middle of the Night was a hit, and Eddie's performance was cheered, along with that of newcomer Gena Rowlands. He was happier than I had ever seen him. And then the old Eddie emerged, commanding the royal treatment allotted to top stars. He came to me demanding a rewriting of his contract, particularly an item regarding the limousine that took him from his hotel to the theater and back.

"Well, Eddie, what's the problem? You do have the limo that your contract requires."

He registered the familiar Edward G. Robinson scowl. "Yes, but it only takes me to and from the theater. I do have to make stops elsewhere, you know."

Eddie defined the word "reprobate." As was his custom, he had several women friends in various parts of the city whom he liked to visit before and after the show.

And so I rewrote Eddie's contract, and in the clause involving the limo, I added the significant phrase "with occasional stops in between." As far as I know, that was a Broadway-contract first. But at least it proved that Eddie was back to his old self.

I loved my Warners period, but various reasons led to my departure from the fold. Among them were J. L.'s truculent nature, wartime gas rationing, and, indirectly, *Casablanca*'s Academy Award triumph.

Casablanca's Oscar victory led to a breakup between J. L. and Hal Wallis. When it was announced as Best Picture, J. L. rushed to the stage to accept the award. Hal, who actually produced the film, justifiably felt he should have been the one who accepted the Oscar, and he left Warner Bros. in a huff. At that time, I didn't realize that Hal's leaving would affect my own future.

During those war years, studio executives traveled in car pools, and I shared rides with producer Jerry Wald. Late one afternoon J. L. suddenly announced there was a sneak preview that evening. None of us had known there was to be a preview, and my car was at Jerry Wald's home. After the preview, J. L. was clearly in a bad mood. Maybe he had heard an ominous "not-so-good" from Abdul. He was seething.

We got into the limo, with J. L. of course in the front seat. Steve Trilling and I sat in back with Charles Einfeld, head of publicity for Warner Bros.

"Who's getting off first?" J. L. asked accusingly, as if getting off first were a crime against studio protocol.

"I'll get off first," I said. "My car's at Jerry Wald's."

"Why should your car be there?" challenged an irritated J. L. "And why didn't you drive your own car, anyway?"

"I didn't know there was going to be a preview," I replied.

Everyone noticed that a trace of hostility had entered my voice. Steve and Charles both clutched my arm, urging me to avoid J. L.'s wrath. But I had definitely been provoked.

"I'll make it easier for you, chief," I said. "Just let me off here. I can find Jerry Wald's house."

"Don't be a fool!" huffed J. L.

"I really prefer to get off here," I said.

Fortunately, I had no problem finding a taxi. When I arrived home, I told Erin-Jo that there might be trouble, and it was possible I would leave Warner Bros. Months earlier, storm clouds had begun gathering over the studio. J. L. had become increasingly testy, and his fury was felt in every office in the administration building. I didn't want to work in that kind of atmosphere, and I wanted to find a position that would bring me closer to producing films myself.

Over the weekend, I packed my gear. On Monday morning, I went back to the studio, to be told that J. L. wanted to see me as soon as I got in. When I arrived at his office, he looked perplexed. He knew that I loved my job, and he felt I would never leave. But his words were threatening.

"You know I can keep you from getting a job anywhere in Hollywood. I only have to make one call, and you'll be ruined in this town."

"I'm sorry to hear you say that," I said calmly.

"Just go back to your office and act like nothing's happened," he ordered.

"But something has happened," I countered. "Something very serious. You just threatened me. I think it's wise for us to say goodbye. And J. L., I'm not afraid of not having a job. You see, I married a girl from Texas."

I wasn't lying. Erin-Jo is from Texas. J. L. in some ways believed the myths perpetrated by Hollywood. To him, the phrase "a girl from Texas" conjured images of vast fortunes made from oil and cattle. In his mind, if you married a Texas girl, you'd never lack for funds, and the threat of unemployment would mean nothing.

Shortly thereafter, I joined Hal Wallis's company. J. L. angrily thought I had the job prior to the ominous night of the preview.

Yet in his later years, J. L. mellowed. In fact, my first personal production *The Hanging Tree* was made for Warner Bros., and so was *The Great Race*. And when he asked me to head the studio's European production in 1964, I happily accepted.

As Samuel Goldwyn supposedly told his secretary: "I never want to speak to that guy ever again—until the next time I need him."

So it was with J. L. And with practically every other studio chief.

2

Prince Hal: The Greatest Producer

~

From Warners to Wallis proved to be a provi-dential move. It gave me the opportunity to work with one of Hollywood's all-time great pro-ducers, Hal B. Wallis, an eccentric gentleman of taste and discretion.

It started with a middle-of-the-night phone call from Prince Hal himself, right after he had left Warner Bros. early in 1944, following the Oscar night brouhaha over *Casablanca*.

"I cannot pay you much, Martin," he said. "But when I do well, you do well. Come over to my house right now and we'll discuss things."

I did well by absorbing his knowledge of all aspects of filmmaking. As for personal finances, he was the stingiest man in town. But what a mentor! I was able to use everything I learned from him in my own productions.

The call from Hal came two weeks after I left Warners. He stressed the fact that we knew each other well and had worked together happily. His right-hand man, Paul Nathan, was away at war, and he asked me to take his place, with the under-standing that Paul would return to Wallis's camp after the war. He named a low salary. But I never regretted my Wallis period. I gained keen insight into one of the sharpest minds in film production.

While at Warners, Hal had supervised such ambitious productions as *Anthony Adverse*, *A Mid-summer Night's Dream*, *Jezebel*, *King's Row*, *Now, Voyager*, and *Casablanca*. After leaving Warners, Hal set up his own production company at Para-mount, a studio that allowed its producers consid-erable freedom as long as they stayed within budget. At Warners, every decision went through J. L., while the Paramount executives were more like business managers.

In his company, Hal was partnered with Joseph Hazen, who had access to much money. We would make six films in eighteen months, an incredible record that included *Love Letters*, *The Strange Love of Martha Ivers* and *Sorry, Wrong Number*.

I devoured all of Hal's contributions, through every step of production. He once said that he could sense a burning sensation in the seat of his

The Hal Wallis staff, 1945. Front row (left to right): Jack Saper, Hal Wallis, Marty, and John Monk. At back: Walter Selzer (left) and Byron Haskin. A happy group, as long as no one expected Prince Hal to pick up the tab.

chair when I came into his office. It was as if I had lit a fire under his chair, propelling him onward so I could sit there.

"I'm not setting any fire," I reassured him. "I just want to learn and to help you."

He was a difficult and remarkable producer. Yet I could not have wished for a more compleat teacher, for Hal B. Wallis was probably the best producer of Hollywood's golden era. While David O. Selznick and Samuel Goldwyn depended a great deal on their department heads, Hal worked assiduously on scripts and had solid knowledge of every aspect of filmmaking.

Eager to find talented newcomers, he was aware of every new Broadway production. One of my duties was to seek unknown talent and bring it to his attention. Between the two of us, we knew the names of every actor who had even one line of dialogue onstage, and I took pleasure in recruiting such future stars as Burt Lancaster, Kirk Douglas, Dean Martin and Jerry Lewis and, much later, Elvis.

Of those young actors, Kirk Douglas seemed to be his own biggest fan, with passions as tense and clenched as his teeth.

Hal and I were casting *The Strange Love of Martha Ivers*, a florid but highly watchable drama with Barbara Stanwyck and Van Heflin. The

KIRK DOUGLAS
IN PARAMOUNT PICTURES

role of Barbara's rich, weak husband was to go to Wendell Corey, a solid actor without the individuality needed for stardom.

Into my office strode a well-chiseled young man full of clenched teeth, full of chin and, also, full of himself. I had already met Kirk and knew he was intense, particularly about Kirk Douglas. But nothing prepared me for his tirade.

"I hate Wendell Corey!" he announced.

"I hate Wendell Corey!" he repeated, as if I hadn't heard him the first time and as if his dislike of poor Wendell made any difference to me.

But he continued on his mission. "He has no business being an actor! You've got to let me test for that part in *Martha Ivers!*"

And so we let Kirk test. Hal and I knew that the role could be a washout unless it was played by an actor of strong presence. Kirk got the part, and Hal used the unsuspecting Wendell in another movie.

In the postwar years, Burt Lancaster and Kirk were often linked as the "terrible-tempered twins." Their reputations were much like Sean Penn's is today, although their behavior was milder.

Burt and Kirk had a friendly competitiveness that, for Burt, lasted to the grave. According to newspaper articles, when Burt was dying, he allowed many visitors in his hospital room but never wanted Kirk to see him. They both were vain about their appearance, and Burt didn't want Kirk to see him looking so ravaged. Knowing that their friendly rivalry could sometimes push the affability envelope, I understood Burt's position. But at least Burt could rest knowing that in all their films together, he was billed first.

It must have been difficult for Kirk to watch his son Michael assume the role of Star of the Douglas Dynasty. Michael has always been gracious about acknowledging his father. But Michael's unofficial father was his *Streets of San Francisco* colleague Karl Malden.

Karl taught Michael valuable personal and professional lessons, which Michael took delight in learning and Karl took delight in teaching. Then, as Michael's star ascended higher and higher, Kirk assumed the father-figure role more eagerly.

Yet, without Kirk, there would have been no *Spartacus*, no *Paths of Glory*, no *Lust for Life* and no *Lonely Are the Brave*.

I had offered to buy *Shane* for Kirk and me to produce. He seemed willing but suddenly said no, without explaining why. He was always convinced that a better offer might be just around the corner. Would he have made a more convincing Shane than Alan Ladd? We'll never know. But he was capable of displaying sensitivity, at least on-screen. And the idea of a shoot-out between Kirk Douglas and Jack Palance titillates the imagination.

There were many sides to Kirk's personality, none of which could be called subtle. In his youth and middle-age, he often seemed like a willful, resentful child, always certain that he was not getting his due while others were getting more than they deserved. I introduced him when he was honored by the USA Film Festival in Dallas in 1976, and he hissed into my ear just before I went onstage, "Don't stay up there too long. They're here to see me."

Yet, old age, which he definitely did not welcome, mellowed him. He and his wife Anne made considerable donations to charity. And he overcame some late-in-life physical difficulties, including a near-fatal stroke, with strength and determination. He even took up writing, and his memoirs and novels won critical plaudits. Kirk's personality was always strong enough to provoke

Kirk Douglas, 1946, the great competitor—while under contract to Hal Wallis at Paramount. (*Dallas Morning News* archives)

contradictory reactions. One of those reactions remains admiration.

Burt was much easier to like than Kirk. Kirk had a bombastic ego even before his work could substantiate it. On the other hand, Burt was simply self-assured. He was also an articulate and honorable man with a sense of humor, even about himself. Much like Katharine Hepburn, he would become involved in all aspects of a film's production. With both Kate and Burt, all their efforts were for the good of the movie, rather than for their own roles.

At the start of Hal's days as an independent producer at Paramount, he had Burt under contract. But, knowing he had little acting experience, Hal never used him. Hal also had the penchant for not picking up an option until the last possible date, in case something happened that made him revise his judgment. In the meantime, Burt, with a face the camera loved, was allowed simply to languish.

At that time, Hal was smitten with Lizabeth Scott, an indifferent actress whose chief talent was taking advantage of Hal's infatuation. Hal said he would test Burt, but a casting director told me it was really to be a wardrobe/makeup test for Ms. Scott, featuring little more than the back of Burt's head. I prevailed upon the director to film full shots, close-ups, and reaction shots of Burt. He did so, and I kept the can of film in my private office, hoping there would be some future use for it. Meanwhile, in Hal's eyes, he had done his duty by the athletic young man who, at that time, was known as Burton Lancaster.

It wasn't long before young Burton Lancaster became Burt Lancaster, movie star. But his breakthrough came at Universal, not at Paramount. Mark Hellinger, then producing films for Universal, had worked at Warners with Wallis and me. Mark

and I became great friends. But he and Hal feuded. Hal could be arbitrary and even haughty in his likes and dislikes. For one thing, Hellinger had been a popular columnist and sometimes made snide remarks about Hollywood. For another, Wallis didn't like the way Hellinger dressed. He wore dark shirts with solid white ties, and Hal didn't like them.

Mark asked me to lunch at Ciro's, a posh Beverly Hills restaurant. He planned to produce a film at Universal from Ernest Hemingway's *The Killers*. One of the lead characters was a tough-but-vulnerable boxer who becomes a pawn in the hands of organized crime. As he described the man's integrity, I thought that he might have been talking about Burton Lancaster himself.

Mark wanted Wayne Morris to play the part but couldn't come to an agreement with Warner Bros. Warners had Morris under contract and had never turned him into a star, but J. L. had no intention of loaning him out with the future options that Mark was demanding.

"Mark, go back to the studio—to your studio, Universal—and call for a projection room," I said. "Send a limousine to my office and I'll plant a can of film in the car. Examine the film. Send it back to me and let me know what you think."

Mark loved Burt's test. Burt's contract with Hal allowed for outside pictures. Hal could do nothing to prevent Burt from doing the film, which would also star Ava Gardner. But before Burt left for *The Killers*, Wallis voiced another objection. He didn't think the moviegoing public could get excited over a name like Burton Lancaster.

When he informed Burt of this, the confident young actor looked directly at him and said, "So call me Humphrey Lancaster! If it's good enough for Bogart, it's good enough for me."

Burt Lancaster, 1946, while under contract to Hal Wallis. . . . A face the camera loved. (*Dallas Morning News* archives)

Burton and I tossed around several possibilities and finally he looked at me and said, "Marty, what do you call me when we're having a casual conversation? What do you call me when we're talking on the phone?"

"Why, I call you 'Burt.'"

"Then that's what it should be. Burt Lancaster."

To tell Wallis that I had given that can of film to Hellinger would have been career suicide. I told him simply that Hellinger had met with Burt and thought he would be great in the role. Hal never knew of the secret screen test.

The Killers was a hit and remained Hemingway's favorite of the many films adapted from his works. And it made the one-time circus acrobat named Burton Lancaster a star for many decades. He was one of the most loyal men in Hollywood, keeping the same agent, a sweet and honorable man named Ben Benjamin, for almost forty years. Like Jimmy Stewart, Burt showed a gift for true friendship.

He loved Italy and enjoyed making such films as Luchino Visconti's *The Leopard*. He invited Erin-Jo and me to visit him there when we were filming *The Pink Panther*, and he seemed happy and relaxed, a former circus acrobat who was a true aristocrat among men. I miss him very much and am grateful that no one took him up on his offer to be called Humphrey Lancaster.

Burt remains one of my strongest Wallis memories, but there are many others.

Barbara Stanwyck was loved by everyone. She was a great favorite of the crew, and her kindness always seemed genuine. But she was nobody's fool.

When she made *The Strange Love of Martha Ivers* for Hal, she had several key scenes with Van Heflin. Van was a talented actor but not a major star, a fact that left a large chip on his shoulder. During rehearsals of an important scene, she

noticed that he kept rolling a fifty-cent-piece through his fingers.

"What are you doing, Mr. Heflin?" she asked.

"Just building character, Miss Stanwyck, just building character," came the answer.

When they shot the scene, he started rolling the coin again. Without missing a beat, Barbara started lifting her dress above her knee, then above her thigh. Heflin's eyes widened and his jaw dropped.

"Just building character, Mr. Heflin, just building character," she explained in the same tones she had used when deliciously teasing Henry Fonda in *The Lady Eve*.

On the next take, he kept the coin in his pocket.

One of my most memorable visual vignettes involved the first day of shooting *Love Letters*, which starred Jennifer Jones, Joseph Cotten and that great wit and peerless character actor Cecil Kellaway. The romantic drama was to be directed by William Dieterle, with a screenplay by Ayn Rand. Jennifer was the pet discovery of David O. Selznick, whom she would marry five years later. David made Hal fume by sending massive memos on how she should be photographed and clothed.

But on the first day of shooting, not a sound came from the soundstage. I went down to the stage and quietly asked the second assistant director what was wrong.

"Don't say a word," he whispered and pointed to a wild spectacle.

At the center of the set was Dieterle, the epitome of a Hollywood director, dressed immaculately in a stylish riding habit accented by a beautiful pair of boots. In the background was violin music. He had ordered a group of violinists to play for Jennifer before each scene, putting the impressionable young actress in the right emotional state.

And off to one side sat the director's wife, lost in contemplation. Mrs. Dieterle believed strongly in astrology. When she felt that everything in the axis was right, she nodded at her husband. Only then would he begin shooting the scene.

Maybe Mrs. Dieterle did know what was in the stars. *Love Letters* was a big hit. But watching the movie wasn't as much fun as watching the filming.

Even without such star-studded memories, I would value my years with Prince Hal as being instructive.

A gifted selector of material, he loved dramatic work like *The Rose Tattoo*, *The Rainmaker*, *Summer and Smoke*, and *Come Back, Little Sheba*. He was a man of infinite taste, even in his private life. He was married for many years to silent screen comedienne Louise Fazenda, but, like all the moguls, he had female friends on the side. He handled those extracurricular activities with decorum, taking pains that Louise would not suspect any liaisons. Around the studio, such discretion earned him the nickname "The Prisoner of Fazenda."

He was demonic when it came to heeding a budget, but his obsession taught me valuable lessons. He studied the blueprints of every set and sought to avoid construction, which was always expensive. For interior scenes, he would often ask, "Do we need a full room? Couldn't we just use an alcove?"

He immersed himself in postproduction, constantly and patiently conferring with the film editor. His films always had an elegant sheen. His strenuous penny-pinching was never obvious to the viewer. But only George Abbott could rival his frugality. When in restaurants, the very wealthy Hal paid for himself only, down to the smallest milkshake.

His only gift to me came after six months, and he obviously considered it a major bonus. It was a bathrobe, designed by Sulka, and it was much too large for me. I paid for the alterations. Did it rankle me? Yes. Did I ever regret working for Wallis? Never.

I never felt vindictive about Hal's lack of generosity. But looking back now, I'm amused that I won an unexpected victory from his deep, largely untapped pockets. My victory occurred after I finished working for Hal, and it came about through the unusual channel of Dean Martin and Jerry Lewis.

I first saw Dean and Jerry onstage in the late 1940s. Erin-Jo and I were enthralled by their zaniness. Their manager was Abner Greshler, a keen agent who specialized in booking acts for the Borscht Belt in upstate New York.

Abner came to me with an exclusive contract for Martin & Lewis's services from MGM producer Joe Pasternak. I had noted—and shared—the tremendous audience response to the team, and I advised against MGM. I brought them to Wallis's attention and spoke to Abner about a nonexclusive contract with Hal. This resulted in a cold stand-off between Pasternak and Wallis, but they signed with Hal. I felt they would be perfect for *My Friend Irma*, Hal's movie version of the hit radio show with Marie Wilson. It became their first film.

I had recommended that their second movie be *A Man in a Box*, based on a vaudeville act about a man onstage being heckled by an audience member in a box seat at the theater. Hal had agreed that if he liked my idea, which he did, he would pay me $10,000. However, he chose *My Friend Irma Goes West* as their second picture. The $10,000 he had pledged me was nowhere to be found, and I sued him.

"You would do that to me?" asked a startled Mr. Wallis, who always expected to be the recipient rather than the giver.

"Yes, I would," was my simple reply.

My attorney, Jacques Leslie, was concerned. "Marty, if you go ahead with this plan, it may be that in the future you will not be doing business with Hal Wallis."

"Let me put it this way, Jacques. In the future, it may be that Hal Wallis will not be doing business with me."

When I sued him, his executives concurred that he should pay me. So I received $10,000 from Hal Wallis. This constituted a major victory.

In any event, it was only a few years later, when I was at William Morris, that I negotiated the sale of the stage hit *The Rainmaker* to Hal for $150,000.

Hal's films earned large profits for Paramount, and one of the studio honchos, Henry Ginsberg, was determined to have him run the studio. But Hal loved his independence, and he was wealthy enough to turn down a large increase in salary. Aside from his earnings in films, he had invested wisely in art and real estate.

A bewildered Ginsberg came to me. "You know Hal so well," he said. "How can we get Wallis to head the studio? Do you have any ideas?"

"Yes, I do, but you probably won't do it."

"What is it? What are you talking about?" he almost shouted.

"The way things work now, whenever Hal wants to watch the dailies of his movies, all he has to do is call for the executive screening room. If someone else has booked the room, that person will be removed so that Hal will get in. But the next time Hal wants the room, simply tell him it's already booked. Give him the name of one of the lowest guys on the Paramount payroll and tell Hal you don't feel comfortable removing this guy from the executive room. Also, Hal gets a massage every day at noon from the studio masseur. Find some way to interrupt his massage every day and . . ."

Henry Ginsberg looked at me and gasped, "Is that the way you think?"

"That's the way Hal thinks," I said. His power and position at the studio were of sublime importance to him.

Ginsberg never tried those tactics. Hal never became studio chief and, as far as I know, never wanted to.

When the war was over, Paul Nathan returned to the fold, and Hal and I parted company amicably. I liked Hal, and we remained friends long after I quit working for him. My indignation over that outsized bathrobe melted into mild chagrin laced with amusement and affection. He was one of the greats.

3

Kate Hep

~

There are legends. And there is Kate Hep. There are survivors. And there is Kate Hep. There are icons. And there is Kate Hep.

The magnificent Katharine Hepburn signed her letters "Kate Hep," and some of her messages are priceless. One recent holiday season, Erin-Jo and I sent her a cheesecake. Her acknowledgment was typically swift and direct.

"Obviously, you haven't read *Me: Stories of My Life*," she wrote, referring to her semi-memoir. "If so, you would have learned without a shred of doubt that I loathe cheesecake. I gave it to a friend who actually likes the stuff. So I was able to save money on a gift."

Outrageous? Not at all. A response like that, coming from anyone else, would give pause. Coming from Kate Hep, it sounds completely in character.

She is like no one else, on-screen or off. She first commanded audiences' attention as John Barrymore's tender daughter in 1932's *A Bill of Divorcement*. For her second role, as aspiring actress Eva

Lovelace in *Morning Glory*, she won the first of a record-breaking four Academy Awards.

Garbo or Dietrich, she was not. Crawford or Harlow, she was not. Aristocratic yet down-to-earth, ostensibly aloof yet filled with compassion, she was the irreplaceable Katharine Hepburn.

Through decades she would be responsible for some of the screen's most enduring images: revealing her shorn hair in *Little Women*, sobbing alone in her room in *Alice Adams*, trying to handle a hangover with dignity in *The Philadelphia Story*, attending her first baseball game in *Woman of the Year*, riding the rapids with Humphrey Bogart in *The African Queen*, inspecting her weary reflection in *The Lion in Winter*, waving farewell to Rossano Brazzi in *Summertime*.

No one else has assembled such a remarkable armory of images. And no other actor has won four Academy Awards. Ever the individual, Kate attended only one Oscar ceremony, and as a presenter rather than as a nominee.

During one of her periodic absences from

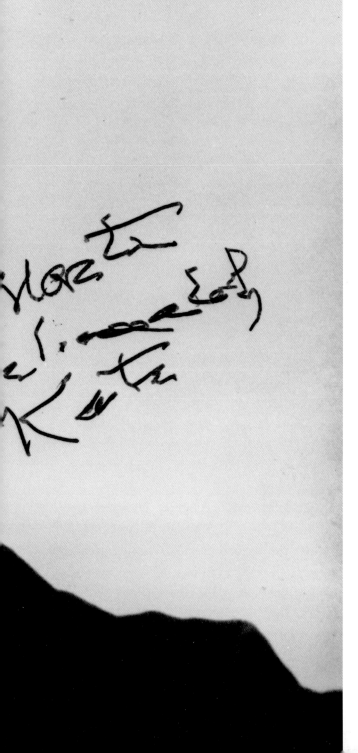

Hollywood, she triumphed with New York and touring productions of William Shakespeare and George Bernard Shaw, adding *The Millionairess, The Merchant of Venice, Twelfth Night, Much Ado About Nothing,* and *Antony and Cleopatra* to her victory list. How many other actors can do justice to Shakespeare and Shaw while carving their own distinguished niche in the Hollywood hierarchy?

When I was head of New York–based motion picture and theater projects for the William Morris Agency, Kate lived most of the year on New York's East Side. She often joked that she meddled in the production aspects of whatever project struck her interest. But it wasn't meddling. As crafty as any bottom-line executive, Kate could read the fine print of the boiler plate agreements issued by studios. She knew exactly what she was entitled to and was determined to get everything that was owed her. She would in fact have made an outstanding producer.

Our friendship took an unexpected turn. She, a professional actress, became mentor to me, hotshot Harvard Law School grad. She pointed out aspects to each contract, explaining their ramifications in diction as precise as her cheekbones.

After her first smash year in Hollywood films, she endured a series of flops that led exhibitors to brand her "box-office poison." One of those flops was *Bringing Up Baby,* later acknowledged as a comedy classic but a commercial disappointment in 1938. Other flops included *Mary of Scotland,* a historical pageant directed by the legendary John Ford, who would become the first great love of her life. Few other actors could survive such a long list of disappointments, but Kate was a master of survival. Sixty years later, when the American Film Institute announced its list of the Hundred

One of a kind, Katharine Hepburn, lifelong friend of Marty Jurow.

Greatest Hollywood Legends, Kate ranked highest among actresses.

Basically a loner, without close Hollywood ties, she was enormously hurt at the "box-office poison" label. She gallantly returned to New York, polished her craft, and honed her public personality. Her friend Philip Barry wrote *The Philadelphia Story* specifically for her, and she scored one of Broadway's most glittering triumphs as all-too-human socialite Tracy Lord.

With the "poison" label still fresh on their minds, some Hollywood insiders felt that Kate should not be allowed to re-create her stage triumph on-screen. It was a great role, and Norma Shearer, still of some importance at Metro even after the death of husband Irving Thalberg, was anxious to play it.

One evening as Kate and I talked while she prepared for that night's performance, she turned to me, her strong features emphatic with resolve.

"Do you know what it is that I should have but don't?," she queried.

"You teach me," I countered. I was always in awe of her business sense.

"The movie rights, and I'm going to get them," she said.

And get them, she did. Many industry people were surprised to learn that Kate literally owned *The Philadelphia Story*. She purchased the play, thus securing ownership of the movie rights. She sold it to MGM—with the provision that she play Tracy on-screen. Louis B. Mayer said that she could make recommendations for the two male costars, and she assured him that she would seek stars of her own magnitude. She settled on two gentlemen named Cary Grant and James Stewart.

The movie's success exceeded the stageplay's, and the first name of *The Philadelphia Story*'s heroine Tracy Lord was to prove prophetic. For her next film, *Woman of the Year*, she also chose her costar, an actor she admired but had never met, an actor whose drowning scene in *Captains Courageous* always moved her to tears.

When she and Spencer Tracy did meet, their personal chemistry was obvious on the soundstage, on the screen, and in their private lives.

The drama of her personal life was of galactic force. She was a magnet for troubled men. She learned early to deal with emotional instability. Her own family members, who constantly rallied around her, sometimes exhibited an erratic grasp of reality. Several members of the family committed suicide, and their tragedies may have heightened Kate's attraction to unhappy men.

This obstinate and strong-minded woman could turn into the most natural of nurturers. Her presence was soothing to such troubled spirits as Vivien Leigh and Judy Garland. And when she made *Suddenly, Last Summer*, she became a lioness in her protection of the faltering Montgomery Clift, whose physical and emotional well-being had deteriorated since a near-fatal car crash.

Howard Hughes, one of the most complex men to walk the earth, was smitten with her. Another love was mercurial agent Leland Hayward, a fastidious man who traveled with many ointments and custom-made suits, shirts, and ties. Theirs was an intensely physical relationship, and when it was over, Hayward supposedly married Margaret Sullavan on the rebound from Kate.

But John Ford and Spencer Tracy were her two great loves. Unlike her relationship with Hayward, her passion for those men was like a meeting of souls. It is difficult to imagine two men with darker spirits. Ford, a great but tormented director; Tracy, a great but tormented actor. Kate loved them both; and they loved her.

Ford was her love during the 1930s, and her love for Tracy lasted from 1942 to his death twenty-five years later.

Ford almost left his wife for Kate but never quite did. Mary Ford was extremely proud of the prestige connected with being Mrs. John Ford and seemed almost demonic in her protection of that rank. She never acknowledged her husband's affair with Kate.

Ford was an elegant, occasionally abrasive man with a love of anything Irish. He had his own group of Irishmen—James Cagney, Pat O'Brien, Frank McHugh, James Gleason—and they enjoyed each other's company in what they called their Thursday Club. But there was definitely a dark side to Ford, one that Kate hoped to soothe.

Ford's truculence was never to be discounted. When he was directing *Mister Roberts*, Henry Fonda, who had played the title role to such acclaim on Broadway, dared make a suggestion. Ford's response was to strike him across the jaw. Yet he welcomed Kate's input on his directing methods, even letting her direct a few scenes. Their respect for each other knew no limits.

Ford suffered from failing eyesight and was terrified at the thought of going blind and being unable to direct. Kate helped him through difficult times. While she tried to soothe Ford, there was no one to soothe her. She was unhappy with how RKO Radio was handling her career, casting her mainly in quaint roles to capitalize on the success of *Little Women*. With *The Philadelphia Story*, she carved victory out of defeat on her own.

Ford and Tracy had similarities. Both were Irish Catholics, forbidden by their church to divorce, and both were volatile alcoholics, hibernating for days, alone with a bottle.

Years after the Hepburn-Ford passion subsided, they remained great friends. Kate got him to

direct Spence in *The Last Hurrah*. I sometimes wondered how this gathering of The Men Who Loved Kate evolved, and I would imagine that Kate did it all by telephone. I remember how Bert Allenberg pleaded with me to talk to Kate so he would have time to talk to other William Morris clients. Kate could talk on the phone for hours, and so could Spence.

Kate would sometimes talk to me about her feelings for Ford. Her voice would soften, and it was obvious that she continued to love him. But that love moved to a different level as her feeling for Tracy intensified.

With Spencer Tracy, her devotion was complete and her commitment unswerving. She devoted her life to him. Tracy, filled with Catholic guilt over his son's deafness, had a mean streak. He was frequently abusive to her when drunk and sometimes even when sober; but she willingly endured his moods. She understood his demons and would gladly have married him, had his religion permitted divorce and remarriage. She even forgave him for not liking her family, and family was sacred to her.

Before he began working on a film, she would visit the sets, making certain the smallest details were arranged to his liking. With him, she was mother, lover, and, above all, friend. Neither Kate nor Tracy sought affection from others, and their love of solitude made them soulmates.

On the set, Spence could be an ornery presence. Like most actors, he did not have time for small talk with the crew. Humphrey Bogart, Burt Lancaster, Gregory Peck, Jack Nicholson, and Marlon Brando all shared that trait. Jack Lemmon is the only major star who enjoys talking with everyone. Kate, of course, could be loquacious, and Spence could be less than gallant when he felt she'd overstepped her limit.

Oddly enough, Tracy loved comedy. Perhaps acting in comedies was his way of finding lightness in his life. He admired Jimmy Durante, George Burns, Fred Allen, and Jack Benny. I know how he must have relished the experience of making *It's a Mad Mad Mad Mad World*.

The cultured director George Cukor, a great friend of Kate and therefore a friend of Spence, built a cottage for Tracy on the grounds of his elaborate Hollywood estate. Spence kept the house almost completely dark and rarely allowed anyone other than Kate or George inside. When Kate visited, she would always light up the cottage, both figuratively and literally.

The house was sparsely decorated, with a kitchen, a pleasant living room and bedroom. In the 1960s, Kate found what she considered the perfect rocking chair for Spence. She liked its contour, its dark blue color and fine fabric. But it was the personal property of an elderly Chinese gentleman who owned a decrepit store in downtown Los Angeles. Kate cared about how she looked and could afford the most expensive shops, but she loved saving money by patronizing stores situated in what some might consider the wrong part of town.

When in California, Kate would visit the Chinese gentleman's shop, but he remained obstinate in his refusal to sell the rocking chair. Each time she saw him, she would embellish her story of wanting to give the chair to a sick man who had only a little time left. She did not realize the truth of what she was saying. Eventually, the Chinese merchant relented and allowed her to buy the chair. When Spence died, she left word with his family that the chair was to be returned to the Chinese merchant. Eventually, they did so, although they were not automatically inclined to accommodate Kate's wishes.

Often Kate would curl up on the floor outside Spence's bedroom doorway, listening for any sign that he might need her. Suffering from insomnia, Spence would read murder mysteries long into the night and then toss and turn for hours. One night Kate finally fell asleep outside his door. At three A.M., she was awakened by a sound and instantly thought, "He needs me!" She opened the door and discovered Spence on the floor, at last finding the peace he had never found in life.

After his death, Kate filled her life with film and stage work. The actress who, thirty years earlier, had been branded "box-office poison" was one of 1968's leading box-office draws, with two major hits in release. *Guess Who's Coming to Dinner?* was her last teaming with her beloved Spencer, and *The Lion in Winter*, in which she was a regal Eleanor of Aquitaine, costarred Peter O'Toole, whom she had recommended to David Lean for *Lawrence of Arabia*.

Except for periodic hibernations when she cared for Tracy or accepted stage roles, she was a vital force in films. She could talk at length about any aspect of show business. David Lean was delighted with her input on characterization and even camera movements when they filmed *Summertime*. Even after directing *The Bridge on the River Kwai*, *Lawrence of Arabia*, and *Doctor Zhivago*, he would still refer to *Summertime* as his favorite film-making experience.

Like George Cukor, who directed Kate in such triumphs as *Little Women*, *Adam's Rib*, and *The Philadelphia Story*, David recognized Kate's ability in all points of filmmaking. They would have long conversations regarding his plans for directing a scene. She would not refer to *Summertime* as "the film," nor anything as colloquial as "the movie." She would call it The Work, speaking with an emphasis that seemed to capitalize the words.

Aside from discussing direction with such film geniuses as Lean and Cukor, she would advise producer Sam Spiegel about casting. She worked with James Goldman on adapting his stage success *The Lion in Winter* to the screen. While filming the sports comedy *Pat and Mike* with Tracy and Cukor, she could play as solid a game of tennis as any pro.

I find it ironic that two of her four Academy Awards are for playing loving mothers in *Guess Who's Coming to Dinner?* and *On Golden Pond*. She never had children, which may have been a blessing. Although she was full of goodness and generosity on her own terms, she never felt she would make a good mother. When not soothing her troubled friends, her focus was entirely on whatever project she was working on. She was capable of impatience and bossiness, and she definitely was not lenient in her judgment of others. Except of course in her judgment of Spencer Tracy. She felt he could do no wrong.

Kate thought I was a trustworthy soul, and by the mid-1950s, I was one of the few allowed into her bedroom. I can still see her New York brownstone. In the entrance was an astonishing array of hats—straw hats, winter hats, summer hats, hats for all seasons. Sometimes I would enter her room wearing one of those hats, to be rewarded by the beautiful sound of her laughter.

When I went upstairs to her bedroom, she might be sitting straight up, her flannel nightgown up to her chin. Near her would be a velour pullover, which she wore over her nightclothes when walking about the neighborhood. Her faithful housekeeper was always in residence.

She would always instruct me to walk to her apartment in order to keep my weight down. And when she invited me for a meal, it turned out to be a sparse lunch in her kitchen. She was such a dear,

peculiar duck. There was nothing wrong with my weight, but a sparse lunch saved her money. Kate could be chintzy and penurious. Yet she frequently sent beanbags to our daughter Erin and velour sweaters to Erin-Jo. I adored her then, as I do now.

During our luncheons, she would unburden herself about her family. She dearly loved both her parents and refused to believe that her older brother had committed suicide. When she was twelve, she had discovered his body hanging in the attic and always insisted his death was accidental.

As far as I know, Spencer Tracy never spent the night at Kate's home. He would visit her privately for hours and then walk back to his hotel. He usually stayed at the Pierre or the Waldorf-Astoria. I would sometimes accompany him on those nocturnal walks, during which he would talk largely of professional matters.

But one evening, he turned and looked back at Kate's brownstone, his eyes brimming with love. "That lady gives me stature," he said, speaking not so much to me as to himself.

I was amazed to hear him utter those words. Even now, I doubt that he ever told Kate face-to-face that he loved her.

Years after Spence's death, Kate came to Dallas with the play *A Matter of Gravity* and stayed at the Stoneleigh Hotel. She and I had dinner together, our hearts filled with glowing memories. After dinner, I told her what Spencer had said. She came over and sat next to me, putting her head on my shoulder. Her face overflowed with emotion for her beloved Spencer.

Later, we walked hand in hand to the elevator. Few words were spoken. Few words were needed. But as I descended to the lobby, I looked upward and said:

"Oh, Kate, you have given me stature too."

4

Sinatra: "He Owes Us"

∾

Before there was Elvis, there was Frankie. Before there was James Dean, the Beatles or Leonardo DiCaprio, there was Frankie.

In the early 1940s, Frank Sinatra was a smash hit as a band vocalist, a radio star, and a recording artist. And when he made a personal New Year's Eve appearance at New York's Paramount Theatre in 1942, throngs of teenage girls, their mothers and grandmothers gathered outside the theater to cheer their hero, who at that point seemed like the king of the world. Police force veterans said they'd never seen anything like it, and many had patrolled the Charles Lindbergh parade.

Some people in the movie industry feared that since he was so skinny, the camera would not love him. But the camera adored him, and his early films were smashes, particularly *Anchors Aweigh*, in which he played a shy sailor who needed Gene Kelly to help him score with women. He didn't need anyone to help him score with women off-screen. All women felt primal urges for him, a sensual longing sometimes mingled with maternal affection. Through the years, his female fans' maternal warmth declined, while their sensual heat escalated.

When Frank Sinatra died in 1998, it was a global event. Some thought of him as a friend and ally, others as a vindictive enemy. But everyone had an opinion of Frank Sinatra, and practically everyone in show business had a Sinatra story. I definitely have a Sinatra story, and it's based on fact rather than lore.

All of us love a good show-biz comeback. It's reassuring to people in the industry. Think of John Travolta in *Pulp Fiction*. Or Ingrid Bergman in *Anastasia*. Or Joan Crawford in *Mildred Pierce*.

No comeback was heralded with more fanfare than Frank Sinatra's in *From Here to Eternity*. It completely revived his career and his confidence, and he remained a star of galactic splendor.

One of the world's great comebacks, Frank Sinatra as Maggio in *From Here to Eternity*, 1953. (*Dallas Morning News* archives)

It's been the subject of fanciful fiction, most splashily embroidered by Mario Puzo in *The God-father*. Even before the pulsating Puzo potboiler, it was a part of Hollywood folklore. As with much of our folklore, very few people know the real truth. I am one of those few.

First we must dissolve to 1953, when the film version of James Jones's dynamic Pearl Harbor novel was in the planning stages. At that time, the performer later known as The Chairman of the Board didn't even rate a good table at a Hollywood restaurant. His last movie, a feeble comedy inanely titled *Meet Danny Wilson*, had bombed. Not all of Frank's films had been smash hits, but they turned a dependable profit. *Meet Danny Wilson* had laid an egg that stank throughout the world.

Frank also owed the government a good deal of money, and his personal life was at a low ebb. He was married to Ava Gardner, and while they would remain friends long after their divorce, their marriage was overcast with thunderclouds. Right then, Frank was torching for Ava, who was in Africa filming *Mogambo* and trying to keep costar Clark Gable's mind off radiant newcomer Grace Kelly.

Frank's voice was gone, his career was gone, and his self-esteem was gone. His voice and career came back. As for his self-esteem, that goes without saying. And it's all due to four words: *From Here to Eternity*.

Fred Zinnemann, the superb director of *High Noon* and *The Member of the Wedding*, and whose later triumphs include *The Nun's Story* and *A Man For All Seasons*, was bringing the massive Jones novel to the screen. He raised eyebrows with the casting of the two female leads—ladylike Deborah Kerr as a lusty army wife and ingenue Donna Reed as a prostitute.

Fred, a good friend of mine and a client of William Morris, was in New York, hoping to cast the superb Eli Wallach as scrappy, doomed Maggio. In case Wallach might prove unavailable, Fred wanted me to help him find the right guy. Maggio was the film's third most important male character, after Montgomery Clift's Prewitt and Burt Lancaster's Warden. But Maggio owned every scene he was in, and the right actor could do wonderful things with the part.

Frank was in Manhattan licking his wounds while Fred, entertaining absolutely no thoughts of Frank Sinatra, was in New York searching for the right Maggio.

At William Morris, the office next to mine was occupied by George Woods, an ebullient, effusive charmer whose specialty was nightclubs. George was friendly with Sinatra. And he was also held in high regard by "quiet investors" in hotels and nightclubs. These "quiet investors" were willing to pay entertainers large fees for performing in their Las Vegas clubs, especially when they realized that most entertainers would gamble away those fees in the casinos.

These illustrious "quiet investors" favored *George White's Scandals*, *Earl Carroll's Vanities*, and various musical revues and plays. They drew the line at dramas. They reasoned that dramas required them to study, while musicals didn't demand serious attention. Besides, they all insisted that their buttocks got tired sitting through a drama.

Frank poured out all his woes to George, who listened sympathetically.

"Let me take you next door to Martin Jurow," George said. "He might have some thoughts."

Because I was head of William Morris's East

Ava Gardner in 1953, while married to Frank Sinatra. (*Dallas Morning News* archives)

Coast film department, George thought I could help.

"That's a tough assignment," Frank told George. "It will take a miracle."

These events occurred on a Saturday, which in itself was a novelty. We used Saturdays for unfinished phone calls and private meetings. As I watched these two men, with their reputed connections to powerful "quiet investors," I sensed this was going to be a very private meeting.

As Frank entered the room, his face and walk showed a wonderful duality that was perfect for Maggio. He was defeated in ways he had never imagined, and his face reflected his despondency. But, even in these dire times, he had an air of resilience and cockiness, balanced with genuine courage.

"What a wonderful Maggio he would make!" I thought.

When Frank saw me, he allowed himself a smile. "I know you, Marty. You sat with me at the Paramount."

I was one of the MCA representatives for Tommy Dorsey when Frank was the vocalist for the Dorsey band. I had been with Frank during that sensational New Year's Eve performance at the Paramount over a decade earlier. Back then, he was just a skinny kid with a magnetic, outgoing personality that exuded confidence but not arrogance. When that show was done, Frank's face showed that he knew something great had happened. But now his face registered only despair.

George and I discussed Frank's professional decline, while Frank remained quiet. That in itself was unusual. Frank was always a great talker. But now that he felt he had nothing to say, his silence spoke volumes.

Without specifically mentioning *From Here to Eternity*, I told Frank, "The best possible thing would be to get you an exciting role in a prestigious picture."

Frank's eyes brightened, and then he repeated what he had said to George: "That will take a miracle."

"Miracles do happen in show business," I said. "So you go on your way, which is probably to Ava, and give me the right to speak for you."

Frank left the room happier than when he entered it.

I had some ammunition. I knew Fred Zinnemann wanted earthy Eli Wallach for Maggio and hoped to borrow him from Elia Kazan's production of Tennessee Williams's *Camino Real*. That night Erin-Jo and I had dinner with Fred and his wife Renee at the Sherry-Netherland Hotel. Over drinks, Fred told me that Eli had a run-of-the-play contract with Kazan, which Fred did not want to interrupt.

"I've got to have a terrific Maggio," he said. "Are there any other ideas?"

"I do have an idea," I said, trying to build suspense in what I hoped was a Hitchcockian manner. "But it requires a man of courage."

Fred was an imposing man, lean and trim from years of mountain climbing. In a quiet voice, with steely eyes, he said, "Do I pass the test?"

"Yes, you do, Fred." And then I said quickly, "With you guiding Frank Sinatra, he will be a perfect Maggio."

At the word "Sinatra," Fred's face turned to stone. His granite silence finally ended, and he spoke.

"Let me explain something," he said. "This is a dramatic film. And Maggio opens the picture. My first shot will be of Maggio leaning on a broom. And you're suggesting I have Frank Sinatra in this part? The audience will see Sinatra leaning on a broom and think it's a prop for a song-and-dance number. They'll think that I've turned *From Here to Eternity* into a musical comedy."

With a slight, teasing smile, I said, "If you can't open a dramatic movie with Sinatra leaning on a broom and not convince audiences that it is in fact a dramatic movie, maybe you shouldn't be the one who directs it."

Because Fred and I were such good friends, I felt I could talk to him as a brother. But total silence greeted my remark. Erin-Jo looked at me. Renee looked first at her husband, then at me. Fred stared solely at me.

"Fred, think of *From Here to Eternity* as a great opportunity for offbeat casting," I continued, under the glare of his stare. "You went through any number of actresses to find the right one to play Karen Holmes opposite Burt Lancaster. Then you cast Deborah Kerr. She definitely has sexuality, but it's not on the surface. And she clicked immediately with Burt."

Fred slowly allowed his face to soften. "It's not a bad idea," he said. "In fact, it may be a good idea. But I don't think you've got a chance of convincing Harry Cohn. But if you get Cohn's OK, I'll put Sinatra in."

Fred and I both knew what Cohn, the despotic chief of Columbia Pictures, would say. He always seemed like the sort of guy who wished he had a loaded revolver in his right-hand drawer so he could shoot anyone who irritated him.

As chief ogre of Columbia, Cohn even surpassed J. L. Warner in levels of tyranny and cruelty. Cohn was treacherous, vindictive, and venomous in ways that no other mogul could equal. His offices at Columbia were fashioned after Mussolini's. The floor around his large desk was elevated, forcing his visitors to look up at him.

By the early 1950s, Harry Cohn was an ailing voyeur, rumored to be impotent, seeking enjoy-

ment by watching others in the act of lovemaking. If Viagra had been available then, he would have bought it eagerly. But only at wholesale.

Naturally, when I called Cohn at his Los Angeles office, I approached him gingerly. I tried to convince him that casting Sinatra in an offbeat role would be a feather in his cap.

Harry's response was typical Cohn. "Put that feather in your own cap, and you can stick it up other places, too," he yelled. "I wouldn't let that bum in my studio! That's all I've got to say, Jur-ra!"

In all the years I knew him, Harry Cohn never pronounced my name correctly.

And then something fantastic occurred, a pivotal plot twist that has been embellished through the years.

That night I wearily went to George Woods's Central Park South home and recounted my woes. Mob leader Meyer Lansky lived nearby. Lansky's aide was Vincent Alo, known to Lansky and his colleagues as Jimmy Blue Eyes. Jimmy would visit George on an almost daily basis before having dinner with Lansky.

Jimmy Blue Eyes wore a dark coat and black fedora. He spoke in quiet tones, and his smiles were brief and hesitant. But nothing escaped his notice.

"What's bugging Marty?" he asked.

"Oh, he's got a problem with Harry Cohn about Sinatra," George said.

"Sinatra, huh? And this Cohn guy, he's the movie guy Cohn?" he said.

So George told him how Cohn was blocking Sinatra's comeback.

"Harry Cohn, huh?" said Jimmy. And then he asked me: "Cohn. Where is he now? In California?"

The way he said "Where is he now?" made me feel like I was right in the middle of an Edward G. Robinson movie.

"Yes," I said. "He's at the studio."

"Does he have a private line?"

"Yes."

"Do you have the number?"

"Yes, I do."

Jimmy Blue Eyes walked over to me and patted me on the head three times. He then spoke with a finality I have never forgotten:

"Cohn. He owes us. Expect a call."

He owes us! Three simple words, but spoken with such ominous certainty. And suddenly I remembered that Cohn was an inveterate gambler. I went home that night knowing that Frank was closer to the part and that I should expect a hostile phone call from an enraged Cohn.

Early the next morning I heard Harry's snarling voice on the other end of the telephone line.

"Great friends you've got, Jur-ra!"

"I don't know what you're talking about, Harry."

"Don't play innocent. You know exactly what I'm talking about. How much do you want for the bum?"

"Well, Harry, his last salary was $75,000 . . ."

"You must be out of your mind!" Cohn exploded, enhancing his statement with a variety of expletives.

"How much will you pay, Harry?" I asked calmly.

"Ten grand. Not a penny more."

I knew he never expected me to accept that amount, and I took pleasure in saying, "I hereby accept. But, Harry, I want you to call Fred Zinnemann and tell him you've okayed Sinatra."

And so Cohn grudgingly called Fred with his OK and then sent me a telegram that succinctly stated "No billing either."

I called the seething Cohn and agreed.

I guess Harry thought it would cheapen the image of *From Here to Eternity* if Sinatra was sold as one of its stars. When it became obvious that Frank was a sensational Maggio, Harry decided to give him billing.

The movie was an instant blockbuster, and Sinatra was showered with laurels. I ran into Cohn and said, "I told you, Harry. It would be a feather in your cap."

He did not answer.

Cohn had not asked for options on Frank, but he should have. Three years later, he would pay Sinatra $150,000 for *Pal Joey*. That made all of us happy.

Who knows what would have happened if Cohn hadn't listened to Jimmy Blue Eyes? But Jimmy didn't have to go to extremes. His powers of suggestion were intimidating enough.

It's all happenstance. What if Eli Wallach had been able to get out of his contract with Kazan? Show business would have been robbed of one of the great comebacks of all time. *From Here to Eternity* not only won Frank the Oscar but turned around his entire career.

He never knew the full story of what had transpired, but he was always courteous to me. Once he looked at me quizzically and said, "I want to pay you back, but you don't seem to want anything from me. You're about the only person who's never asked me for anything."

"You've given me your trust, Frank," I said. "That's all I require."

A year later, when I had to tell him that Marlon Brando, and not he, would star in *On the Waterfront*, I was grateful for his goodwill. The look in his eye was unnerving, but he accepted the situation with grace.

Still, he was a man of many moods—vicious and violent, generous and gentle. Like anyone who is overly aware of his position and demands constant recognition, he was not always pleasant company. He sought to eliminate anything disturbing or displeasing to him. His physical presence was commanding. You could sense it as soon as he walked into a room. You also sensed that if he happened to have a gun, he would be perfectly capable of using it.

He could be a charming host. He enjoyed his image and never objected to picking up the tab. He always treated his parents well, and his mother, a strong woman, was a dominant figure in his life. Frank loved many women. With his marriage to Mia Farrow, he gained the interest of the powerful youth movement of the 1960s.

In what seemed like an odd coupling of pals, Frank had great regard and affection for Gregory Peck; their friendship lasted until Frank's death. I always believed that while Frank might not admit it, he patterned himself after Greg. Both men dressed elegantly, but Greg has the height that Frank lacked.

On both professional and personal levels, Greg passed tests of character. Can the same be said of Frank? My mind jumps back to an evening early in my relationship with Greg when I was driving through the byzantine Hollywood Hills for dinner at his home. Always plagued by a fear of heights, I found myself getting dizzy and stopped at a phone booth to call Greg and tell him what had happened. He insisted on picking me up and driving me personally to his house, which was still far away.

Would Frank have done the same? Or would he have told me to take a leap off a cliff? It would all depend on his mood, and he was definitely a man of moods.

Frank Sinatra's talent and mystique will endure beyond his death. His phrasing of lyrics made him a master musical interpreter, and his intensity made him a first-rate dramatic actor. Frank often gave the impression that he thought he was the universe, and maybe he was. Certainly he was a prince. A tarnished prince, rather than a noble monarch. But a prince nonetheless.

To Erin Jo
and Marty.
Love,
Eva Marie

5

Waterfront

~

The behind-the-scenes drama of *On the Waterfront* starts not on the New Jersey docks but at a Beverly Hills poolside. And it was a drama that carried reverberations even in 1999, when the classic film's brilliant director Elia Kazan was awarded an honorary lifetime achievement Oscar.

The Beverly Hills Hotel was a wonderful place to make deals. Pretty and pink, it featured the illustrious Polo Lounge as well as a gallery of poolside cabanas where movers and shakers conferred in a relaxed atmosphere. But that day in 1954, when William Morris Agency president Abe Lastfogel and I met with Elia, he was anything but relaxed. Elia was almost always called Gadge, short for Gadget, due to his propensity for using his body as a tool, attaining various contortions to make his point. That day, every inch of Gadge's body was filled with tension.

When Gadge went to California, Abe was his channel. In New York, I would service Gadge's needs. I always serviced them quickly, knowing

that he is not a patient man. On this particular afternoon, Gadge was frowning ferociously, without saying a word. Abe and I tried to extract from him some reason for his dolorous mood.

Finally he told us. 20th Century Fox titan Darryl F. Zanuck had turned down *On the Waterfront*, which Gadge desperately wanted to direct. The drama had a terrific screenplay by Gadge's friend Bud Schulberg. Bud was the son of B. P. Schulberg, who was a decent man and one of the film industry's pioneers. Gadge already had earned prestige and profits for Darryl's company with *Gentleman's Agreement*, *Boomerang*, *Pinky*, and, most recently, *Viva Zapata* with Marlon Brando. But Darryl felt there was no audience for a film dealing with waterfront unions and crimes.

"I'll do anything else you want," Darryl had told Gadge. "Just name another picture and you can do it."

"I want to do *Oedipus Rex*," Gadge said facetiously.

Eva Marie Saint and Marlon Brando in *On the Waterfront*, 1954. Eva Marie still remembers their improvisational love scene.

"Are you crazy?" Darryl exploded. "We're not doing *Oedipus Rex!*"

As Gadge finished his tale of woe, I noticed a man hovering nearby, devouring every word. He was Sam Spiegel, known earlier in his career as S. P. Eagle. He had produced *The African Queen* in 1951 but had followed that smash hit with a huge flop. *Melba*, the biography of opera star Nellie Melba, starring the Metropolitan Opera's "baby diva" Patrice Munsel, had played to empty houses. He was at a low ebb. But, being a man of chutzpah, he put on a happy face as he walked over to greet Gadge. He got right to the point, pleading with Gadge to let him produce *On the Waterfront*. He was certain he could get studio backing.

Abe, knowing that Spiegel was not on any studio's A-list, said simply, "Let's think about this." He was not head of the William Morris Agency for nothing.

Sam persisted. "Give me a month! Just a month! I'll bring you a deal from a studio. I know I can do it! But first I should read the script."

That was typical of Sam Spiegel. A consummate dealmaker, he was ready to negotiate without even having read the script.

I returned to New York, where I continued to work with Sam on the project. Once he read the script, he felt fairly optimistic. He and I both felt that the principal role of tough/tender Terry Malloy spelled Marlon Brando. Sam never doubted for an instant that he could get Brando, whose career had zoomed with *A Streetcar Named Desire*, directed by Kazan on stage and screen. Also, with Marlon Brando heading the cast, studio backing would be a cinch.

It didn't quite turn out that way. Two studios passed on the project, feeling the subject matter was too depressing and uncommercial. Finally I had a secret meeting with Harry Cohn, who now

treated me more courteously, since *From Here to Eternity* had been a record-breaking Oscar-winner. Harry felt that maybe *On the Waterfront* would be a film that Columbia could be proud of, and Spiegel was in a state of euphoria.

That feeling turned to despair when we suddenly learned that Gadge and Marlon were not speaking to each other. Marlon was outraged by Gadge's activities during the Joe McCarthy era of blacklisting. Even forty-five years later, the controversy surrounding Gadge's naming of names had not been soothed. When the Motion Picture Academy of Arts and Sciences voted an honorary Oscar for Gadge in 1999, some members felt it was an insult to those who had been blacklisted. I did not participate in the backstage drama of that Oscarcast, but I know it must have been fiery. Gadge and I never discussed politics. I knew him only as a brilliant artist.

Both Marlon and Gadge were in agony at this point. Marlon left word with Sam and me that he was no longer involved in the project, that he would never again work with Elia Kazan. Marlon was vehement. Gadge was sensitive, confused, and hurt.

Very wearily, Sam once again put on a happy face and assured Cohn, "We're working on it." For all his frailties, Sam was not a man to give up.

I now called Abe Lastfogel, saying that I felt I could talk Harry Cohn into using somebody else.

"Who?" asked Abe.

"Frank Sinatra," I said.

So I called Harry, and when I suggested Sinatra, he paused briefly and then said, "I agree."

One year can make a great deal of difference in show business.

I then called Frank, telling him that if the rupture between Marlon and Gadge continued, he might play the lead in *On the Waterfront*. Frank was elated, knowing it would be an unprecedented feat to follow *From Here to Eternity* with *On the Waterfront*.

Nobody ever knew that I made that call. In fact, Gadge never even knew that Frank was close to getting the part. We were waiting for the right time to tell him, and he was still upset from the tension with Marlon.

And then came another phone call, this time from a very happy Spiegel. "Martin," he said. "Come to the St. Regis Hotel. I have something to tell you."

When I got to Sam's suite, I noticed the door on the other side of the room was closed.

"They're inside that room," he said.

"Who are?"

"Marlon and Gadge. They've made up. They're back being best friends. Now isn't that great?"

"But Sinatra's on his way to New York this very minute. What am I to tell him?"

"That's your problem," Spiegel said with a wave of his hand. "You want me to go in there and ask Marlon and Gadge to stop speaking to each other again?"

Possibly, Abe himself had arranged for Marlon and Gadge to be reunited. He had a great knack for getting people together. He might have called Gadge and said, "There's only one way to break the ice with Marlon. You make the call. Just you, not your representative."

The *Waterfront* dilemma could have brought a bravura display of the famous Sinatra temperament. But when I called him to my office and told him what had happened, he was extremely decent. He seemed to understand that, despite his own urban background, Brando might be the better choice for *On the Waterfront*'s Terry Malloy.

As he turned to go, he stopped suddenly and said, "I still think the script is great. So why not let me play the priest?"

For the moment, he forgot that when he played a priest in *Miracle of the Bells*, the movie was one of the turkeys that threatened to end his career.

"I'm sorry, Frank," I said. "The priest is filled. Karl Malden will play him."

For an instant, Frank looked hurt. Then he nodded and left the office.

Aside from Frank, everyone was elated. Harry Cohn was pleased to have Brando, and Sam Spiegel had gotten a start that would launch him into becoming one of our most important producers, with such films as *The Bridge on the River Kwai* to his credit.

I had seen Eva Marie Saint onstage in *The Trip to Bountiful*, and I felt her luminous quality would be perfect for *On the Waterfront*'s female lead. Her fair-haired ethereal face would be in contrast to Brando's more primitive features. At my urging, Gadge went to see her onstage and was immediately impressed. He sent for her and told her he wanted her to improvise a scene with Brando. Eva Marie remembers every detail of that event, sharing them in a recent letter that provides insights into Kazan's style of working:

I have no idea what Gadge said to Marlon, but he was very specific about my action in the scene. He told me that Marlon was my older sister's boyfriend. He was coming to see her, but she was not at home. I was the only one at home and under no circumstances was I to let him in.

Well, all I know is that no matter what I said, Marlon got in the front door. We ended up dancing together. Marlon was very charming,

Letter from Eva Marie Saint to Erin-Jo Jurow, February 12, 2000.

and I couldn't resist his charms. Gadge saw the sparks fly between us. I would love to know what he told Marlon before our improvisation. After that improvisation, the part was mine. It was all very clever of Gadge. I shall never forget that improvisation because it was thrilling to work with Brando and Gadge."

Like Brando, Kazan and the picture itself, Eva Marie won an Oscar. Eva Marie and her husband, Jeffrey Hayden, remain good friends with Erin-Jo and me.

A year or so later, Gadge, Tennessee Williams, and I were at the Sherry-Netherland bar. I had arranged the meeting. Gadge and Tennessee had reached an impasse in preparing *Cat on a Hot Tin Roof* and were not speaking. They sat apart from each other at the bar and never looked at each other. I would go from Gadge to Tennessee, carrying messages from one to the other. I repeated each message verbatim. When the clouds finally cleared, we compared notes. I had one version of the messages. Gadge had another version. And Tennessee had yet another. Any creative process is a little bit like Rashomon. People hear what they want to hear and read what they want to read.

Marlon and Eva Marie were only the beginning of *On the Waterfront*'s unforgettable cast. I've always considered Karl Malden a poster boy for personal integrity. He was a great help to Gadge, who trusted his insights completely.

I love all actors, but some of them fit snugly into types. Lee J. Cobb, as the union boss, and Rod Steiger, as Brando's brother, were stalwart fellows, tough guys looking out primarily for themselves. I seldom spoke to Cobb, who was far from approachable. Instinctively, I felt he was the type of actor it's best to know onstage rather than offstage. But I spoke a great deal with Rod, who was obviously trying to develop a rapport with someone who might be helpful to him in the future. Rod played his cards cleverly in his attempts to nurture valuable relationships.

On the Waterfront brought dividends to all players. But subsequent years were not always kind to Marlon. He often made bad choices of material and sometimes didn't play fair with people. But his mere presence could dominate a scene. Yet at times, it seemed something was missing.

Compare Brando's performance in *The Godfather* with Walter Huston's in *The Treasure of the Sierra Madre*. Brando's is sheer showmanship, a virtuoso visual performance, whereas Huston's is great visually and aurally. For twenty-four days, while I was touring with *Boy Meets Girl*, I went to a theater in Boston just to hear Walter Huston sing "September Song" from *Knickerbocker Holiday*. His delivery was wrenching, and he didn't need facial gimmicks to aid his performance. That's a great actor.

Many of the people involved in *On the Waterfront* are gone now. Even Gadge, formerly a whirlpool of energy, is an old man now, confined to his home.

But the result is still with us. *On the Waterfront*, which Darryl F. Zanuck rejected as being uncommercial, remains a celebrated and important film, a story of warmth and humanity.

Would Frankie have been as convincing a Terry Malloy as Marlon was? We'll never know. My instincts tell me, probably not. But it's still an intriguing "might have been."

6

Elvis

≈

In my work, I've felt moments of electricity, moments that are wonderful to experience, relive and cherish.

I felt that electricity when I watched a young Gene Kelly strut to the stage for an audition, when I saw understudy Shirley MacLaine perform on Broadway, and when I met George C. Scott in person.

But nothing compares with watching Elvis Presley's New York rehearsal in January of 1956.

Usually, when you spot an exciting talent, the vibrations start at the ankles and travel right up to the head. When I watched Elvis, the sensation went from ankles to head, through the ceiling and out into the atmosphere over the New York skyline. I knew that something significant was about to happen in the entertainment world.

It was a rarity—this rock 'n roll music and this young man named Elvis Presley.

And it began with the kindness of others. Life

at the William Morris Agency was harmonious. Everyone enjoyed helping everyone else, and this goodwill extended to our clients. One of our clients was Andy Griffith, one of the most generous-hearted men in the business.

Andy had told my friend and associate Harry Kalcheim about this entertainer from Memphis with the unusual first name of Elvis. On Andy's recommendation, we booked Elvis on the Dorsey Brothers' television show. As I knew from working with them at MCA, Tommy and Jimmy Dorsey were always feuding. But the battling bandleaders were able to endure each other's company when they cohosted the replacement show for Jackie Gleason's hit series *The Honeymooners*. At William Morris, we convinced them that a little rock 'n roll might swing the ratings upward.

Harry came into my office and urged me to head straight for Elvis's rehearsal. I agreed immediately. From all I had heard, I felt that Elvis Presley's

Already electrifying—Elvis Presley, 1957. (*Dallas Morning News* archives)

future possibly did not rest strictly with recordings, live performances, and television.

The rehearsal was to take place at Nola's Studio, which was right above Lindy's famous deli. Having skipped lunch, I stopped at Lindy's and got a sandwich, intending to munch on it while I listened to the Memphis Kid. Looking back, I laugh at my blase attitude. Why, sure, I'd just watch this new kid between bites of corned beef!

At the studio, I met the future king, one of the politest young men I've ever encountered. Greeting this well-mannered, deferential individual, I had no idea what I would experience once rehearsal started. But as I watched him perform, electricity filled the air. He sang, he swiveled, he rocked, he rolled.

I had the wonderful sensation of witnessing something completely new, a blending of music and personality unlike anything that had come before. Sinatra had been a superb singer and a stunning personality. But Elvis was the harbinger of a new musical style. If only his unique qualities could be captured on-screen!

Never noticing that my once-important corned beef sandwich had dropped to the floor, I immediately called four executives from various film companies, singing Elvis's praises as vigorously as he had sung for me. I advised them to watch the young entertainer on the Dorsey Brothers' show Saturday. One of those executives was my own ex-employer Hal Wallis. The others were heads of 20th Century Fox, Columbia and Metro-Goldwyn-Mayer. All said they would call me Monday morning.

That was a historic evening, that Saturday night of January 28, 1956. Erin-Jo and I sat mesmerized, our eyes glued to the television. That night, Joe Hazen, Hal Wallis's New York representative, would notice that his nineteen-year-old

niece had shredded her fine French handkerchief while watching Elvis. All across the nation, everyone felt the same electricity.

The King of Rock 'n Roll would also prove to be a king of machismo. But while his macho movements were aggressive and provocative, they were never oppressive or bullying. Women responded to him with a mixture of adoration and awe. Rather than feeling threatened by him, men wanted to emulate him.

Early Sunday morning Hal Wallis called to say he was ready to make the deal then, that he wouldn't wait for Monday morning.

I had wanted Hal to sign Elvis all along. But I didn't want Hal to know he was at the top of my wish list. I knew he was a producer of taste and intelligence albeit of mind-boggling stinginess. And I thought it essential that Elvis be allied with a producer of undeniable taste. Otherwise, I feared, he might become Elvis the Freak, with his swiveling pelvis the subject of all camera angles.

I was actually glad that when Elvis made his sensational appearance on the Ed Sullivan Show, he was photographed only from the waist up. On-screen, he would certainly get his share of close-ups, and I wanted to see if he could thrill a crowd with the emphasis on his face and music rather than on his pelvis.

The initial movie negotiation was one of the few facets of Elvis's career that his notorious manager, Col. Tom Parker, did not steamroll. Later, Col. Parker sought complete control of his hot property. But at that time, he was shrewd enough to realize his inexperience with the movie world and allowed me to negotiate with Wallis.

That was fine with me. I never liked Col. Parker. He was a con artist, a medicine man, and, above all, a parasite. I never detected any personal feeling for Elvis on his part. He thought of the King of Rock 'n Roll as property and nothing more. He owned 50 percent of Elvis, and Elvis simply did as he was told.

Col. Parker always would claim that I sold Elvis out to Hal Wallis. He always thought Hal gave me a bonus for bringing Elvis to his attention, which shows how little he knew Hal Wallis.

Wallis allowed me to help supervise Elvis's screen test. Not a natural actor, Elvis would always need, and welcome, attentive direction. But his face and personality came across so vividly, he might well be a major star. Even Hal didn't know how major.

At William Morris, our negotiations with Wallis were intensive, and he finally agreed to our demands. We wanted $15,000 for Elvis's first movie, doubled to $30,000 for his second. And I insisted on a privilege that was rare in those days. I wanted Elvis to be able to do one movie each year away from the Hal Wallis banner. That really made Hal squirm, but he grudgingly agreed.

As it turned out, Elvis's first movie was not for Wallis. It was *Love Me Tender*, at Fox. And during the three-month interim, Elvis had become such a phenomenon that we were able to increase his salary from $15,000 to $250,000, plus 50 percent of the profits. That's what I call growth stock! No wonder I still feel indignant that the Colonel claimed I had sold out to Wallis.

A couple of years later, Elvis came to me and discreetly suggested that I might produce a film for him. I instantly said no. I knew that Col. Parker and I could never share the same meeting room, soundstage, or lunch table without getting into a shouting match. He and I would never be able to agree on the same project for his profitable property.

Shortly thereafter, early in 1958, I tried to per-suade Arthur Penn and Fred Coe to cast Elvis as Billy the Kid in *The Left-Handed Gun*, with its off-beat Gore Vidal screenplay. But they were sold on Paul Newman. Paul is a wonderful actor, but I felt Elvis might more readily suggest Billy's childlike qualities.

It's an understatement to say that many of Hal's pictures with Elvis were not artistic triumphs. Hal frequently alternated prestige pictures like *Come Back, Little Sheba* and *The Rose Tattoo* with projects designed simply to be moneymakers. I wish Hal had viewed Elvis as a prestigious per-former rather than merely a profitable one. As it was, Elvis had fun, fun, fun with girls, girls, girls in Acapulco, Hawaii and Las Vegas. The movies often seemed interchangeable. Whether *The Left-Handed Gun* would have steered Elvis's career in a different direction, we'll never know.

Elvis's musicals were inexpensive to make and didn't require a massive audience to turn a profit. Probably 95 percent of the lightweight Elvis musi-cals were heavyweight moneymakers. Hardly any other star could make that claim. Like Frank Sinatra and Judy Garland, Elvis proved an aston-ishingly durable performer, one whose life became a legend.

He and I lost track of each other through the years. He made fewer films, but his fans delighted in his spectacular Las Vegas performances and his phenomenally successful tours.

I heard the same stories everyone did, about his binges of food, drugs and alcohol. As I thought back to the polite gentleman who greeted me at Nola's Studios in New York, I tried to convince myself that those stories were exaggerated. I would love to think that the sweet-souled young man at the rehearsal still existed beneath the burden of celebrity.

7

Judy at the Palace

~

The world of popular entertainment is filled with unforgettable moments, all wondrous examples of the right performer at the right place at the right time.

I feel proud, or more accurately, I feel honored that I took part in one of the century's grandest personal performances—Judy Garland's personal appearance at the Palace Theater in Times Square, which became known as *Judy at the Palace*. She opened there on October 16, 1951, and it was a legendary event.

So much has been written about Judy Garland, yet it's almost impossible for words to capture the essence of this remarkable, lovable, maddening, contradictory, and completely human woman. She was as sweet and as tough as they come. She was an outstanding artist whose wrenching voice captivated audiences. Her voice was always full of heart, even as she battled the heartlessness of drug addiction.

Think of the parade of songs automatically associated with her name: "Over the Rainbow," "The Trolley Song," "The Man That Got Away," "Have Yourself a Merry Little Christmas," to name just a handful.

Yet for all her triumphs, she ultimately was a victim. She enjoyed her victories but always wondered what mishap awaited her.

In her later years, Judy became an extremely edgy woman. But as a teenager during the late 1930s at Metro-Goldwyn-Mayer, she was anxious to please. And studio chief Louis B. Mayer was the one whose approval she tenaciously sought. He was a father figure, he was her Papa Louie.

He became a very demanding father.

Her early years at Metro were largely happy. She adored Mickey Rooney and loved working with him in *Babes in Arms*, *Babes on Broadway*, *Strike Up the Band*, *Girl Crazy*, and several Andy Hardy comedies. Those movies' make-believe fam-

When Judy Garland sang, the world sang with her. (Photo by Wm. Langley, *Dallas Morning News* archives)

ilies became her surrogate family. But Mayer over-worked her cruelly and advocated medication to ease her exhaustion, tension, and depression. The dependency on medicine evolved into a dependency on drugs.

And it was father figure L. B. who fired her in 1950 from the movie version of Irving Berlin's *Annie Get Your Gun*. From 1939 through 1948, she had made classic musicals for the studio—*The Wizard of Oz, Meet Me in St. Louis, The Harvey Girls,* and *Easter Parade,* in which she gave a delightful comedic performance. But L. B. thought her behavior too erratic to be trusted with the rigorous role of Annie Oakley, and he borrowed Betty Hutton from Paramount to replace her. Judy wept bitter tears, feeling desolate and betrayed.

As I look back, I realize that a search for some sort of family was a vital part of Judy's emotional makeup. Estranged from her own kin, she relished the support of friends. Friendships at least allowed happiness on an immediate, short-term basis. She was at her most spontaneous and vibrant when performing before a group of peers, doing an impromptu number at a party.

During the late 1940s, Sunday dinners at the Beverly Hills Hotel were formal occasions, considered happy rituals by the stars. Whoever was present would perform. Mickey Rooney and Phil Silvers did a hilarious interpretation of "Ole Man River." And Judy made everyone weep with "Over the Rainbow." No party that Judy attended was complete until she had done a medley of her songs.

On one of those memorable Beverly Hills Hotel evenings, after Judy had given a particularly moving performance, Erin-Jo witnessed Judy stretched out on a divan in the ladies' room, drinking whiskey out of a silver flask. She was only twenty years old.

Judy also was a great audience, truly appreci-ating the talents of others. She depended upon the goodwill of her peers, and I am sure that it pained her to be Oscar-nominated for 1954's *A Star Is Born* and lose to the younger Grace Kelly. Her peers were among the Academy voters, and Judy must have been devastated.

Like most people who sense a void in their lives, she sought marriage. Again and again. She thought and hoped she would be a successful wife, and for a while she was. Her first marriage in 1941 was to David Rose, a quiet, handsome, affable bandleader who loved playing for Judy. Erin-Jo and I spent our first social evening in Hollywood at Judy and David's house, when agent Swifty Lazar invited us to join him at their home. They were warm and gracious hosts and seemed devoted to each other.

Her second marriage, in 1945 to director Vincente Minnelli, was initially serene. She respected him, and he was a warm soul who had her interests at heart. But she could never be happy for an extended length of time. She would pretend to be, but her friends could see through her pretense.

She brought out protective instincts in people. Early in 1951, when Judy was performing at the Palladium in London, I was with her when Katharine Hepburn came backstage. Kate was departing for *The African Queen* location, and Judy was trying to regroup from the *Annie Get Your Gun* debacle. By that time, Judy's drug dependency was common knowledge within entertainment circles.

Kate was like a compassionate older sister who understood her little sister's frailties and loved her all the same. They both laughed when Kate told Judy that she planned on wearing no makeup in *The African Queen,* and that all freckles would be exposed. Kate felt that her decision would please Spencer, and it comforted Judy to know that someone as strong as Kate should seek the approval of another. Kate's kindness to Judy came naturally. Kate respected talent, and few artists had more talent than Judy Garland.

But drugs clouded Judy's judgment when it came to men. Witness her rendezvous with Joseph L. Mankiewicz and her later marriage to Sid Luft. Mr. Mankiewicz, director and screenwriter of *All About Eve*, briefly became her coach, her tutor, her mentor, and her lover. Above all, he was a supreme egomaniac with an eye for women. His choice of studios was determined by his choice of women. He made his greatest films for 20th Century Fox because Linda Darnell, the object of his lust, was a Fox contract star. Judy's relationship with such a man hardly helped her self-esteem.

Sid Luft was an ex-pilot who wanted to navigate all of Judy's professional and personal choices. But his attempts at navigating seemed more like interloping. By that time, Judy was more determined than ever to make her own decisions. To put it mildly, their temperaments were not well-suited.

After I saw Judy's London success, Abe Lastfogel and I were trying to think of an American showplace suitable for her enormous talent. A light came into Abe's eyes, and he said four simple words that would create a Broadway legend: "Judy at the Palace."

The Palace, located at Broadway and 47th Street, was the New York mecca of vaudevillians, and every artist in the early part of the century longed to play there. After the vaudeville era ended, it was a mixed-use venue, sometimes for personal appearances, sometimes for movies. But the Palace remained a legendary showplace, the perfect setting for a sparkling gem like Judy. It had been the theatrical home for Al Jolson, Sarah Bernhardt, and Eddie Cantor during the teens, the 1920s, and the 1930s. And now it would be a mecca for Judy Garland.

The problem was that Sid Luft didn't want the Palace. He wanted the Metropolitan Opera House and already was negotiating with the Met.

Abe was incensed, and so was I. We met with Sid in the suite he shared with Judy at the Plaza Hotel. Words volleyed back and forth. Abe might be furious, but Luft was adamant.

And then, from behind a closed bathroom door, came Judy's unmistakable voice crisp, terse, and final. "The Palace, Sid, the Palace."

Despite Luft's interlopings, Judy's was the deciding voice. Her legendary show lasted at the Palace for nineteen weeks and could have played for a year had other contracts not intervened. Always one of the hardest workers in the business, she collapsed from exhaustion, and performances had to be cancelled for two nights. But the sell-out crowds and sensational reception helped restore the confidence she lost when she was fired from *Annie Get Your Gun*. And her final performance at the Palace, on February 24, 1952, was an unforgettable event. She received the ovation she deserved—which veterans said was the greatest, most heartfelt ovation in Broadway history. And we in the audience, with tears in our eyes, joined Judy in singing "Auld Lang Syne." None of us will ever forget that moment.

I made frequent backstage visits to the Palace, and we had lively chats. She was witty and clever but could be a fierce opponent when necessary.

She showed nothing but love for her daughter Liza Minnelli. Liza's godmother was the incomparable Kay Thompson, singer, composer, writer, musical arranger, pianist, producer, and radio star. As Liza grew up, Judy would strongly encourage her to work with Kay and absorb her vast knowledge.

Kay's death in 1998 received surprisingly little notice. Her career was enormously far-reaching. She wrote the best-selling book *Eloise* about a precocious, lovable brat who lived at the Plaza Hotel and played matchmaker to the guests there. When Kay was asked how she managed to cover such a wide range, she said words that probably soothed the complex natures of Judy, Liza, and countless other show folk: "Work hard. Have a sense of humor. Look for comfort. And very often look for tra-la-la. Don't take things too seriously."

I was part of Kay's representation, and I would help bring the Williams Brothers, one of whom was Andy, onstage with her.

If Judy was your friend, she was loyal and steadfast. And I think the same must be true of Liza. Kay had been reclusive prior to her death, which occurred, in varying reports, at the age of either ninety-two or ninety-five. When she died, she had been living with Liza, who had offered her warmth and comfort. For that brand of loyalty, I salute both Judy and Liza.

Judy inspired loyalty, and Abe Lastfogel was the most loving of agents and the most loyal of fans. To him, clients were champions worth cherishing. He was their agent and their cheerleader, a trait that gave the William Morris Agency a more personal touch than MCA.

Shortly before his death, Abe continued going to his office, but his razor-sharp mind wandered, and his eyes had a listless look. His wife Frances had preceded him in death, and he often seemed lonely. He would sit alone in his office, which had only one decorative touch—a painting of a clown with a sad face.

But when I came to see him, his eyes became more focused. "Tell me about it, Marty," he would say. "Tell me about Judy at the Palace."

And I would happily recount our negotiations with the Palace, our arguments with Luft and how Judy cast the deciding vote from the bathroom. And I would describe the impact of the legendary show, with its unforgettable closing night.

A big smile would fill Abe's face, and his eyes would become luminous. Everytime I told him the story, he would get up off his chair and hug me.

He had never forgotten what it was like to sing "Auld Lang Syne" with Judy Garland. And neither have I.

8

Lullaby of Broadway

≈

Few excitements in show business equal that of the opening night of a Broadway show. While I love the art of the cinema, live performance is to me the most personally seductive form of entertainment.

Through my years with MCA and William Morris, I was privy to the creation of the words and music of the masters. The agencies represented someone in every Broadway show. In my mind flows a wonderful montage of musical memories, enhanced by a hit parade of Broadway melodies.

During my tenure there, MCA represented Richard Rodgers, who became a dear friend. One of my most vivid memories is of a time when he was bereft and almost desperate. His first partner, the talented and tormented Lorenz Hart, had died. Together, they had created wonderful scores for *Jumbo, Babes in Arms, I Married an Angel, The Boys from Syracuse,* and *Pal Joey,* which made Gene Kelly a star.

But in the early 1940s, with Larry Hart gone, Richard was filled with sorrow and doubt. He was

definitely uncomfortable with any kind of self-doubt. He and I had lunch in midtown Manhattan, and he expressed his sense of personal loss and his sudden lack of professional confidence. As we left the restaurant and walked along a crowded Park Avenue, he apologized for being such doleful company.

"Dick, there's a wonderful passage in the Bible," I said. "It says 'To set at liberty them that are bruised.' Let's liberate you, Dick. You can keep on going. And you can do more than just keep on going. With your talent, you'll find a new partner and go to new heights. You'll go higher and higher."

By mere happenstance, I had used the right phrase. *Higher and Higher* was the name of a show Dick had written in 1940, and his lips slowly curled into a smile. After Larry Hart died, Dick and Oscar Hammerstein joined forces and became the most successful creative team in Broadway's musical history.

In 1951, eight years after their groundbreaking musical *Oklahoma!,* we were involved in the tantalizing production of *The King and I*. It was trying out in Boston, and the show was going to be closed without even reaching Broadway. The lustrous Gertrude Lawrence, who starred as Mrs. Anna, was partners in the production with Rodgers and Hammerstein. She had asked them to create a musical based on *Anna and the King of Siam*, but now she wanted to shut the show down.

Gertrude Lawrence was a formidable talent and a formidable woman. Like her dear friend Noel Coward, she was the epitome of British sophistication. Born in poverty, she worked her way up, first as a professional dancer. Eventually she fulfilled her strongest dreams and became the toast of both London and Broadway, with such shows as *Oh, Kay!*, *Tonight at 8:30*, *Private Lives*, and *Lady in the Dark*.

And now she wanted to close *The King and I* out-of-town. Yul Brynner's magnetic performance as the King of Siam was stealing the limelight. But the real problem was her voice. She had been performing since she was twelve, and her voice was now strained and limited. Dick couldn't even bear to listen to it. Gertrude was overwrought with tension.

When I came to Boston, representing Gertrude and her attorney Fanny Holzman, there was intense backstage turmoil. Gertrude and Dick were not speaking to each other. And Dick was not speaking to me. He knew I was a friend, but at this juncture he felt I was in the enemy camp. His silent rage at Gertrude could explode at any moment.

Oscar Hammerstein filled me in on everything, emphasizing the fact that at midshow intermissions, audiences raved about Yul rather than Gertrude.

"She needs a showstopper in her first act," I said. "And then she will be praised at intermissions as much as Yul is."

Oscar's face clouded as he thought of creating a song for someone whose voice could not rise to many challenges.

"She needs a showstopper, and she needs it soon," I prodded.

Oscar suddenly relaxed, the clouds disappearing from his face. "I think I have the right song."

Years before, he had written "Getting to Know You" for another show, only to discard it. He now resurrected it, and he placed in the context of Mrs. Anna singing to the King's many children. And, most importantly, the children would join in the singing. Gertrude's limitations would be covered by forty Oriental children. Gertrude was smart enough to know that the children were used to camouflage her shortcomings and wise enough not to object. She died the following year, her remarkable career ending triumphantly with *The King and I*. Thank heaven for those forty Oriental children.

As for Yul, he played *The King and I* for 4,257 performances. He owned the role while he was alive. But after he passed on, a revival showcased an extraordinary performance by Lou Diamond Phillips, a gifted young actor few thought had the makings of a King of Siam. The story of *The King and I* continues to be a magnet for creative artists, although the 1999 nonmusical movie *Anna and the King* was a definite disappointment for Jodie Foster.

What great outpourings of music came from Rodgers and Hammerstein!

South Pacific opened before *The King and I* and was instantly judged a masterpiece. Mary Martin and Ezio Pinza were perfectly cast in the leads. I

Angela Lansbury was a dream, on the stage, on the screen, and in private life.

was part of Ezio's representation. He moved across the stage with leonine grace, and Mary, who washed her hair for three minutes each performance during "I'm Gonna Wash That Man Right Out of My Hair," was radiant and charming.

Mary exuded lightness and confidence onstage, but she was a natural worrier. She made her Broadway debut in 1938 with *Leave It to Me*, in which her delivery of "My Heart Belongs to Daddy" created a sensation. She became a top star in 1943's *One Touch of Venus*, but she fretted constantly about not being the right height to play a diva goddess. But once she started singing, no one cared about her height. Still, she worried about not being right for any show in which she was cast, while her husband, producer Richard Halliday, offered reassurance.

Thirty years after *South Pacific*, I approached Horton Foote to produce a movie version of his haunting *The Trip to Bountiful*, starring Mary Martin and her son Larry Hagman as the play's mother and son. When I suggested the idea to Mary, she was adamantly opposed to it. When I tried to reason with her, she grew firmer.

Finally, she said with a touch of wounded dignity, "I'm not old enough to play that part."

And that was that.

Like *The King and I*, *Guys and Dolls* would be revived on Broadway to unanimous acclaim. We represented Abe Burrows, who wrote the book. Composer Frank Loesser would later write thirty-three songs for *The Most Happy Fella* and score yet another triumph with *How to Succeed in Business Without Really Trying*.

Guys and Dolls ruled the stage, but it was a pauper in its screen translation. Not only was Frank Sinatra cast as Nathan Detroit when he would have been perfect for Sky Masterson, but the direction by Joseph L. Mankiewicz was incred-

ibly lumpish. A man of talent and ego, Mr. Mankiewicz could not find the right visual style to transfer a stageplay into a movie. Neither could the gifted Fred Zinnemann, whose screen version of *Oklahoma!* was a disappointment. Mervyn LeRoy had trouble capturing the magic of *Gypsy*, and Vincente Minnelli flopped with *Brigadoon*. Generally, Hollywood's best musicals were not based on Broadway shows. Created for the stage, Broadway musicals often don't translate to other media.

I was involved in many facets of Cole Porter's *Can-Can*. Our client Abe Burrows directed the show and wrote its book. The producers simply told him that they wanted a musical that took place in Paris at the end of the nineteenth century. He took those instructions and came up with *Can-Can*.

The French import Lilo was the star of *Can-Can*. I found her French accent too heavy and felt she should be replaced, but when the show lasted over nine hundred performances, I was glad the producers, Cy Feuer and Ernest Martin, hadn't taken my advice. Lilo was good, but the show was stolen by the sensational dancing of Gwen Verdon, who would make Broadway history in *Damn Yankees* and *Sweet Charity*.

The production of *Pink Tights* starred Renee "Zizi" Jeanmaire, the French ballerina and singer known to movie fans primarily as the actress adored by Danny Kaye in Samuel Goldwyn's *Hans Christian Andersen*. Piquant rather than traditionally beautiful, she was usually billed only by her last name. Erin-Jo got delightfully suspicious when Jeanmaire and her mother kept inviting me over for French snacks after the show.

One evening Jeanmaire had dinner with us at a quaint rural inn in Connecticut. We all ordered fried chicken. Jeanmaire casually asked Erin-Jo, "What would you do if someone went after Martin?"

My fork was poised in the air, but Erin-Jo didn't miss a beat. She uttered one crisp word—"Acid!"—and went right on eating her chicken. End of discussion.

Actually, Jeanmaire had fallen in love with choreographer Roland Petit when she was ten years old and they were chums at a Paris ballet school. But Roland now was attracted to someone of his own gender, and she didn't know how to tackle that problem. At that time, Roland and the young man were working in Las Vegas, and Jeanmaire asked my advice.

"Go to Las Vegas immediately. Hold him, love him, kiss him, engulf him," I said, and then I tried some balletic phrases for effect. "Spring toward him in a pirouette and envelop him in a passionate pas de deux. Throw your wonderful legs around him in a sissone. Let no one separate you. Show him what your love can do."

A short time later, Western Union delivered Jeanmaire's message from Las Vegas. It contained only two words, "La victoire!"

Zizi and Roland were soon married. And they remain so.

The Pajama Game was one of the most enjoyable successes of my career at William Morris as chief of East Coast motion picture and theater departments. The night I saw Shirley MacLaine go onstage for the ailing Carol Haney was an enchanting evening that led to her Hollywood stardom. Every aspect of the show was filled with talent. George Abbott co-wrote the book, with music by Richard Adler and Jerry Ross. Mr. Abbott and Jerome Robbins co-directed and Bob Fosse was choreographer. Looking back, the thought of how much great talent was involved in *The Pajama Game* is staggering.

And the producers were my protégés from the Abbott days—Robert Griffith and the extraordi-nary Harold Prince, demonstrating a vision that would make him the greatest director of Broadway musicals. He always valued our time together and autographed a book for me with the words "To the Coach." I often wish Hollywood had taken advantage of Hal's great talent. If so, I am certain there would be a larger number of successful movies made from Broadway musicals.

The Music Man was a superb show, a slice of Americana that had trouble getting financing. Its creator Meredith Willson was no musical novice; he had composed the score for the much-lauded movie version of *The Little Foxes* and often worked as a conductor. But some producers wondered if Broadway theatergoers would show up for a musical that took place in Iowa. I reminded them that audiences eagerly stood in line to see a musical that took place in Oklahoma.

I was in Las Vegas on business when Meredith called me, begging me to hear his *Music Man* score. And so, in a small room in Las Vegas, accompanied only by a piano, Meredith serenaded me with the entire show of *The Music Man*. The magic of "Seventy-Six Trombones" and the delicacy of the rest of the score were mesmerizing.

I convinced the great director/librettist/playwright Moss Hart and his wife, singer and TV star Kitty Carlisle, to come hear what Meredith had wrought. Erin-Jo would be present at the meeting, to lend nervous Meredith moral support.

On a cold, snow-swept night, Moss and Kitty, both usually the epitome of graciousness, arrived at Meredith's apartment. But when they started to listen, the temperature in that room dropped by at least fifty degrees, making it colder inside than outside. Their sophisticated tastes were immune to the musical's charms, and they left in a perfunctory manner.

Meredith and his wife Renee were disheartened and almost yielded to the temptation of turning *The Music Man* into a television special. I knew that the show was too good to simply be a one-shot TV special. And I felt that the key to its success would be to find the perfect "music man." I suggested Robert Preston, and everything fell into place. Bob had only been a second-tier actor in films, but his personality and vocal delivery were ideal for the stage. His electrifying performance as Professor Harold Hill pulsated for 1,375 performances. It was a perfect match of actor and role.

The Music Man was simply not Moss's type of show. As a couple, Moss and Kitty personified soigné. In 1956, Moss beautifully directed *My Fair Lady*, the instant classic that he considered the hallmark of his career.

My Fair Lady's legendary success began with a phone call to me from Gabriel Pascal. He owned the movie and stage rights to all of Shaw's works and asked me to meet him at his athletic club. In a sauna atmosphere, he said he wanted me to represent him as he produced *Pygmalion* as a musical.

Gabriel and I both thought the imperious Rex Harrison would be a natural Henry Higgins. Ironically, Rex had to be cajoled to take the part. Knowing of his amorous private life, I prevailed upon both Gabriel and the show's producer Herman Levin to get both Rex's wife Lilli Palmer and his amour Kay Kendall to prevail upon Rex. It worked. A young and very appealing Julie Andrews, whom American audiences had adored in Cy Fueur and Ernest Martin's revival of *The Boy Friend*, would play Eliza.

Alan Jay Lerner and Fritz Loewe's music for *My Fair Lady* would be heard across the globe, and the musical would be applauded worldwide. But Gabriel Pascal would never see his dream realized. He died before the show opened on Broadway.

Like Hollywood, Broadway was populated by a caravan of real characters. Ethel Merman was a belter who proved her prowess from *Panama Hattie* to *Annie Get Your Gun*, from *Call Me Madam* to her brilliant dramatic and musical performance in *Gypsy*.

But much to her dismay, she lacked the necessary magic for movies. She was dynamic onstage, but the camera didn't love her. I tried hard to get her into films, and she made the movie version of *Call Me Madam*. She wept bitterly when the film was not a hit. She watched *Annie Get Your Gun* go to Betty Hutton, and she was heartbroken when Rosalind Russell was cast in the movie version of *Gypsy*.

The undeniable fact that Ethel lacked what the camera desired completely shook her up. She was in top-tier company. Mary Martin, Gertrude Lawrence, Katharine Cornell, Tallulah Bankhead, Julie Harris, Carol Channing, Alfred Drake, Alfred Lunt, and Lynn Fontanne all triumphed onstage but rarely on film. Either their features didn't photograph strikingly, or their acting styles were too theatrical.

One of my most enduring professional relationships was with Jule Styne, who wrote the music for *Bells Are Ringing*. Its star was the talented and troubled Judy Holliday, whom I represented. Judy had problems with her weight, and I had problems trying to help her keep her weight down. Weight control was a factor in her contract, and Erin-Jo and I became her breakfast-time caretakers.

In New York, we lived at the Dakota, the oldest apartment building in the city, where Judy also lived. Knowing she would never have diet food in her home, I convinced Judy to have breakfast with Erin-Jo and me. Each morning, she would take the back elevator to our apartment, and Erin-Jo would serve hard-boiled eggs instead of the bagels and cream cheese Judy craved.

Judy insisted that she faithfully followed the Harper's Bazaar diet, which consisted solely of steak, tomatoes, spinach and hard-boiled eggs. But we suspected that her determination diminished by the time the dinner hour arrived.

On Broadway, Judy had created the memorable Billie Dawn in *Born Yesterday*. She was even asked to do the movie version, for which she won the Oscar over such outstanding co-nominees as Bette Davis in *All About Eve* and Gloria Swanson in *Sunset Boulevard*. Still, she was always nervous, always skeptical of her success. She couldn't quite believe she was a major star, but she always wanted to make sure everyone else believed it. She went through life like an uncertain but tyrannical shopper who terrorized the salespeople.

Tragically, African-American performers suffered in show business as they did in other professions. Lena Horne, a beautiful and gifted entertainer, played to sell-out audiences in plush New York supper clubs. But the owners always insisted that she change clothes downtown. In the 1950s, they didn't want a black woman using their dressing rooms. I tried to get them to change their minds, but they refused. To their eternal credit, Danny Kaye, Hildegarde, and Milton Berle refused to perform until the situation was corrected.

Sammy Davis Jr. was one of the most exuberant talents in show business history. As Sidney Poitier was to the movie world, Sammy was to the stage. They were both courageous pioneers, and their success spoke to African-Americans everywhere.

Onstage, as singer, dancer or impersonator, Sammy was stunning. At William Morris, we were convinced he should break with the Will Mastin Trio and go out on his own. This wasn't easy; the trio consisted of Sammy, his father, and his uncle.

Sammy didn't think he was ready. But, more than that, I think he was afraid to say anything. His father and uncle had been with him all his life, and he felt they would never want to be shorn of the act. Finally, at a hotel in Philadelphia, I told him he had to leave the trio for the sake of his career. We finally convinced his father and uncle that Sammy should go solo. Not an easy task, even after Sammy promised to continue paying them full salary. They were only too happy to extract that promise from Sammy, but I always wondered if they truly wished him well. After the trio disbanded, they never spoke to me, and Sammy rarely spoke of them.

I felt the time was right for Sammy to make his appearance in musical theater. I convinced Jule Styne to produce Sammy's Broadway debut, and I take a small credit in coming up with its title, *Mr. Wonderful*. Jerry Bock co-wrote the music and lyrics. Joseph Stein, who would be of great help to *No Time for Sergeants*, co-wrote the book. Jack Donahue directed. *Mr. Wonderful* opened in March of 1956 to mixed reviews. But there were raves for Sammy, and for talented newcomer Chita Rivera.

Shortly after his success as Mr. Wonderful, Sammy's life took an unexpected detour. He was in a Palm Springs car accident one night, resulting in the loss of one eye. Naturally, he was devastated. Electrifying in person, Sammy longed, as so many others did, to be a movie star. Sammy had so much talent, as well as an honest desire to share it with the public. He had harbored fantasies for his starring debut in films, loving the idea of playing a jockey. He said he was built like a jockey. He dreamed of doing westerns and had learned to ride horses and carry a gun in his holster. Now those roles were impossible. His car accident relegated him to sidekick characters.

Sammy also was one of the most loyal people in show business. When Humphrey Bogart lay dying of cancer, he was a constant attendant. And

in Sammy's eyes, Frank Sinatra could do no wrong. Frank gave Sammy a strong position onstage during concerts with Dean Martin and himself back in the Rat Pack days. Onstage with Frank and Dean, Sammy enjoyed an equality rare for an African-American entertainer in the late 1950s.

One thing about Sammy disturbed me. As his actions toward his father and uncle indicated, he was a generous person. He also loved to live lavishly and often found himself without funds. I tried vainly to convince him to get a financial advisor.

Always, I was amazed at Sammy's talent. And I still think we didn't see enough of that talent. He wasn't an easy commodity to sell to the movies, and his film appearances were rare outside of the Rat Pack comedies. He started concentrating almost exclusively on recordings because they paid well and spotlighted his individual vocal style. For those of us lucky enough to have his recordings, few joys are as exuberant as hearing Sammy Davis sing.

Angela Lansbury remains a consummate artist. She's an amazing actress, a wondrous personality and, as a human being, she's a champion. All her roles—in film, theater, and television— became jewels. Think of her when she made her movie debut in the Gothic drama *Gaslight*. She was only nineteen years old but held her own with such towering talents as Ingrid Bergman and Charles Boyer. Eighteen years later, she gave a deliciously sly performance as Laurence Harvey's seductive mother in the classic *The Manchurian Candidate*— despite the fact that she was only three years older than he.

The stage provided the best showcase for her talent. She was stunning in *Mame*, a particularly significant feat since some observers felt that Rosalind Russell, who starred in the nonmusical *Auntie Mame*, owned the role. And in a revival of *Gypsy*, she wrapped her multitude of talents around Mama Rose, a role so closely associated with The Merm. Angela had another offbeat character and another triumph with *Sweeney Todd*. With the smash success of *Murder, She Wrote*, she became a welcome guest in the nation's living rooms.

I worked with her husband Peter Shaw at the William Morris Agency, and at various times, we both represented her. He's an endearing man, with a keen combination of streetsmarts and intellectualism. Had I remained an agent, I would have been proud to fight the good fights for Angela. She's a beloved figure. When Angela and Peter visited Dallas in 1999, we spent hours together reminiscing.

On Broadway, as in Hollywood, I learned early never to underestimate a star, never to consider a star to be finished. An ostensible has-been can spring back to vivid life. Many of these Broadway pros were turbulent human beings, but I loved them. And I thank all of them for making my lullaby of Broadway so happy.

The Will Mastin Trio, composed of (left to right) Will Mastin, Sammy Davis Jr., and Sammy Davis Sr. Sammy Davis Jr. was generous to his partners, as he was with everyone. (*Dallas Morning News* archives)

9

London Days

~

I've always been an Anglophile, loving England's literature and artwork and admiring the British perseverance sometimes described as "stiff upper lip."

My London memories consist of two chapters, one in the mid-1950s when I was with William Morris, the other in the late 1960s, when I was head of European production for Warner Bros.

Looking back on my London days, they're a montage of faces and places, picturesque and lively, haunting and indelible. One face stands out in the montage, that of filmmaking genius David Lean, with whom I enjoyed an enduring friendship.

I was David's U.S. representative, and I had loved his works since that day in 1945 when I saw his unforgettable *Brief Encounter*. It was a poignant romance, filmed in realistic settings and starring Celia Johnson and Trevor Howard. In 1993, I read that maverick director Robert Altman, responsible

for M*A*S*H and *Nashville*, decided to become a filmmaker after watching it. I understood why. *Brief Encounter* was not about Beautiful People. It was about human beings.

David Lean favored exotic locations and exotic women. But for all his fascination with landscapes, he also loved the architecture of the human face. He photographed Alec Guinness, Katharine Hepburn, William Holden, Peter O'Toole, Omar Sharif, and Julie Christie with ardent appreciation, placing their faces against breathtaking backdrops. His films have both stunning vistas and stunning visages.

On *Summertime*, which he filmed in 1955, the conferences between David Lean and Kate Hepburn were wondrous to behold. He had never worked with a star of her magnitude and didn't know what to expect. What he got was a woman as direct and strong-minded as he. In fact, com-

David Lean won an Oscar for *The Bridge on the River Kwai*. Sophia Loren was the presenter. (*Dallas Morning News* archives, AP wirephoto)

pared to Kate, he was reserved and shy. This lover of exotic women found a soulmate in New England's own Kate Hepburn.

For *Summertime*, Kate convinced him that she should do her own stunt of falling into the Venice canal. When she suffered ongoing infections from the filthy water, David regretted his decision. Kate, ever the perfectionist, did not.

David had a showmanly fondness for intrigue. At William Morris, I was his spokesman when he came to the United States from England. We never met anywhere as prosaic as an office or a hotel lobby. He preferred street corners with picturesque names. He loved to meet near Washington Square, with its Henry James resonance, or at Gramercy Park, where thirty years later punk rocker Sid Vicious would take his own life. A simple business meeting would resemble an espionage rendezvous.

He made two of his most famous films—*The Bridge on the River Kwai* and *Lawrence of Arabia*—for the mercurial Sam Spiegel. Sam had not changed greatly in the two years since the turbulent start of *On the Waterfront*. He was the same old Sam, a dangerous charmer and master manipulator. But in his own mind, he had changed. He felt he had become High Society and tried to cultivate the Beautiful People. It is an understatement to say that David and Sam were not temperamentally well-suited.

I spent hours listening to David's complaints about Sam and always understood his viewpoint. Sam's moods would alternate between bullish confidence and noisy panic. David was obsessive about his work but never abrasive.

He and I decided on Ceylon as the perfect location for *The Bridge on the River Kwai*, partly because he wanted to stay as far as possible away from Sam's intrusive eye.

The location shoot of *The Bridge on the River Kwai* went smoothly. David revered Alec Guinness and admired William Holden's ability to boost the crew's spirits with humor and kindness. Holden's role had been written for an Englishman, but Lean was happy he cast the all-American actor in it. Spiegel was happy, too, from a box-office point of view.

But that was one of the few things they agreed on. They argued constantly, and had Spiegel spent more time at the location, things would have gotten explosive. The day after *The Bridge on the River Kwai* swept the Oscars, David wrote me a touching and tender letter, thanking me for my understanding of his situation with Spiegel.

Next was David's triumphant study of Lawrence of Arabia. International film circles had a new guessing-game: Who would play the enigmatic T. E. Lawrence? Any actor deemed remotely suitable was mentioned. At times it seemed like everyone except John Wayne was in the running.

In the casting of *Lawrence of Arabia*, David's friendship with Kate Hepburn paid dividends. She admired a young actor named Peter O'Toole, whom she had just seen in a West End comedy. She felt he looked right for the part and was convinced of his talent. So she recommended him to David. When Kate and Peter made *The Lion in Winter* five years later, I wondered if he knew of Kate's part in his career breakthrough.

Of David's three epics—1957's *The Bridge on the River Kwai*, 1962's *Lawrence of Arabia*, and 1965's *Doctor Zhivago*—*Doctor Zhivago* received the least enthusiastic reviews. Some critics too quickly dismissed it as a Russian soap opera. But it became a huge hit, the *Titanic* of its day. It appealed to all demographics long before "demographics" became a buzzword of movie marketing teams.

Five years after *Doctor Zhivago* came *Ryan's*

Daughter, beautifully filmed in Ireland. Sarah Miles played the tempestuous heroine but was unable to summon the epic-sized passion of Julie Christie in *Doctor Zhivago*. However, Robert Mitchum was memorably cast against type as a gentle school-teacher. The critics, possibly still resenting the *Zhivago* phenomenon, bashed *Ryan's Daughter* as a slight tale embellished only by stunning visuals. It was the first real disappointment of David's career, and he was devastated.

Always a loner, he embraced solitude more fully than ever. In 1986, fifteen years after *Ryan's Daughter*, he bounced back with *A Passage to India*. It was well-received critically and created a nice stir at the box-office. But a nice stir doesn't compare with the thunderous acclaim David had grown accustomed to.

At least before he died, he got to witness the successful reissue of *Lawrence of Arabia*, and a photograph of David's reunion with Peter O'Toole and Omar Sharif made all the papers. With the reissue, David's complete filmography was reevaluated in glowing terms. His exquisite camera work was lauded, and *Lawrence of Arabia*'s magnificent introduction of Omar Sharif crossing the sands was deemed one of the screen's greatest visuals. I know how happy David must have felt when he read the critical praise.

He was a strange man, capable of love but craving solitude. Although his epics required enormous crews, he was happiest seeking his own counsel. I liked and respected him. Sometimes I even understood him. But not always and never completely, which probably is just the way he wanted it.

~

My second London chapter occurs in the 1960s, during the period known in the annals of pop cul-

ture as Swingin' London. And swing it did, with worldwide impact.

On any popular London street corner, you might find Twiggy posing for photographers or Julie Christie hiding from them. Mick Jagger could be found almost anywhere in the city, giving the impression that he didn't care if anyone took his picture. Designs created on Carnaby Street in London's fashion district were the rage. Miniskirts ruled. James Bond movies reigned internationally. And the sounds of the Beatles filled the air.

I had just finished *The Great Race* at Warner Bros., and, unlike the old days, Jack Warner and I got along well. Jack had mellowed, and the fact that *The Great Race* was sure to be a hit put him in a pro-Jurow frame of mind. He offered me a position in charge of European production for Warner Bros.

I knew it would not be a lengthy stay. I could tell that Jack was tired, and I suspected something that once would have been unthinkable, that he was searching for a way to sell the studio. But while in London, the Jurows had a grand time.

In the 1960s, celebrities often took up residence in London for tax benefits. It became a refuge for blacklisted talents like Michael Wilson and the much-wronged Carl Foreman. Jules Dassin and Melina Mercouri, the brilliant but blacklisted husband-wife team responsible for the comedy hits *Never on Sunday* and *Topkapi*, also found a haven there.

Across the world, the 1960s saw a mixture of the old and the new. In some countries, including parts of America, the two generations collided fiercely. But in England, they mingled in friendly, colorful ways.

The names of provocative British writers like John Osborne, Harold Pinter, and Robert Bolt made strong impacts. Yet England also remained the country of the classics. I can visualize the West

End ablaze with the latest Pinter or Osborne, blissfully coexisting with revivals of Shakespeare's tragedies and Oscar Wilde's comedies.

England was presenting the world with a new vision, a new design and a new challenge. But its arts scene demonstrated how the old and new could be united by sheer talent. Albert Finney, Richard Harris, Alan Bates, and Oliver Reed were voices heard throughout the continents. These fresh, sometimes brash new artists mingled with such veterans as Sir Alec Guinness and Sir Ralph Richardson. Yul Brynner was in London exuding a personal charisma that captivated all his colleagues. David Niven, Rex Harrison, and I often had tea at the Connaught Hotel. Rex was wry and witty, yet capable of seeming aloof and even snobbish. His self-absorption was enormous, even in a profession where self-absorption is a given. But when he was with David, he relaxed and seemed a completely pleasant chap. David's sense of humor made people feel mellow and satisfied rather than competitive. He enriched the lives of everyone around him.

Gregory Peck visited London at various times, making *Arabesque*, directed by Stanley Donen and costarring Sophia Loren, and filming parts of *The Guns of Navarone* there. At every visit, both Yanks and Londoners treated him with awe. He was respectful of everyone and therefore respected by everyone.

In London, much of the entertainment world frequented a club/restaurant called the White Elephant. I was always amused at the thought of myself, the producer of *The Pink Panther*, dining at the White Elephant. It was there that I convinced the talented British director Peter Yates to cut his salary and go to San Francisco to direct a Steve McQueen thriller. *Bullitt* became Steve's signature film.

As much as Americans tried to assimilate into British life, we welcomed each other's company. Every Sunday, the Yanks would gather for softball. I can still remember all the greetings: "Hey, Beatty!" (Warren) . . . "Hey, Brynner!" (Yul) . . . "Hey, Simon!" (Neil) . . . "Hey, Gelbart!" (Larry).

There was such camaraderie in those Sunday softball games. All of us felt like we were partners in a great adventure, in a London lark.

Some of the visiting Americans tried to be more British than the native Londoners. Stanley Donen, director of such American classics as *Singin' in the Rain* and *Seven Brides for Seven Brothers*, had married Lady Adelle Beatty, whose previous husband had been Lord Earl Beatty. By virtue of his marriage to titled aristocracy, Stanley was considered a role model. Everyone had to have a chauffeur. Producer Irving Allen, making the Matt Helm caper *Murderer's Row* with Dean Martin, lived like a member of the landed gentry. He owned a stud farm, which bred thoroughbred horses. Once, at an afternoon party at the farm, I tried to smile obligingly at an approaching stallion, but I really wanted to run and hide.

During my time in London, one of my greatest contributions to Warner Bros. did not involve a film shot in England. Instead, it was a movie that was filmed in and around my future hometown of Dallas, Texas. The movie was *Bonnie and Clyde*, and it was Warren Beatty's obsession.

Warren had scored a hit in his 1961 debut opposite Natalie Wood in Elia Kazan's *Splendor in the Grass*. But his follow-up movies, even Tennessee Williams's *The Roman Spring of Mrs. Stone* with Vivien Leigh, had not capitalized on his initial impact. One of his biggest flops had been the moody, allegorical *Mickey One*, directed by the gifted Arthur Penn. He was now in London making *Kaleidoscope* for director Jack Smight, whose Paul Newman private eye flick *Harper* had been a hit for Warners.

I had read the screenplay of *Kaleidoscope* and felt that, with Warren at his most charming, it could be an enormous success. It required him to play an ingratiating con artist, a part in which he could be very convincing.

Warren spoke of the film he wanted to make in Texas about bank robbers Clyde Barrow and Bonnie Parker. He hoped to produce and star, with Arthur Penn directing. But Jack Warner and Ben Kamelson, head of studio distribution, scorned the idea of making a film about vicious criminals, even though Warners had been a leader in producing "tough guy" movies with Bogart and Cagney.

Warren used his considerable powers of persuasion to convince J. L. that the film was an homage to the studio's earlier gangster pictures. But Jack barked back, "What the devil's an homage?"

During this time, I was in California for a brief visit and spent an hour convincing Ben that, with *Kaleidoscope* certain to be a smash, the studio should invest in Warren's upcoming movie.

Kaleidoscope went nowhere at the box office. Although, at my urging, *Bonnie and Clyde* was made under the Warners banner, the studio initially did not really support the movie although critics loved it. Warren, nothing if not resolute, begged, pleaded, and cajoled Ben to re-release it with a different campaign. It was a smash hit, launching Warren as a major Hollywood power player.

Ever the charmer, he would refer to me as his champion. My misguided enthusiasm for a made-in-London caper called *Kaleidoscope* had paved the way for the American classic *Bonnie and Clyde*.

The film brought director Arthur Penn new prominence. I had known Arthur for years, first in live television and then as the Broadway director

who guided Anne Bancroft to glory in *Two for the Seesaw* and *The Miracle Worker*. He would follow *Bonnie and Clyde* with the haunting, picaresque *Little Big Man* with Dustin Hoffman. In the spring of 1999, we visited when he came to Dallas to be honored by the USA Film Festival, and we reflected on old times. *Bonnie and Clyde* is one of the great American movies. But when I think of it, I always think of London.

For much of our time in London, we lived in a three-bedroom flat on Eton Square. Vivien Leigh had been living there when she died. When she and Laurence Olivier were married, their love was so strong and sincere, you felt it would never end. Even after their divorce, they could not stay away from each other. Larry would stop off at Vivien's flat to dress for his performances. Regardless of any turmoil in her own life, she would greet him lovingly.

Raquel Welch asked to use our London home for her wedding pictures, and we gladly obliged. Her wedding to Patrick Curtis had taken place in her own apartment, which she felt was too small for wedding pictures. I've read all the negative press about Raquel, presenting her as a temperamental, arrogant diva. But Erin-Jo and I remember her as an ambitious yet sweet young woman, taken aback at the sexism and male chauvinism that's often rampant in the film community.

At one point, I flew to Rome to talk Raquel into coming out of her dressing room. She had locked herself inside because she felt her director was treating her as a sex object rather than a serious actress.

While there, I visited with Elizabeth Taylor and Richard Burton to discuss future projects. They assumed that I had come to Rome only to see them. In their eyes, that was more than adequate reason to make the journey.

Elizabeth made a point of deferring to Richard, anxious to present him as the master of all matters relating to show business. She reminded me of dear Audrey Hepburn, so self-effacing while building up Mel Ferrer. Both women wanted their husbands to feel that they were as professionally important as their wives. But neither husband was deluded for long.

Several years later at New York's Lombardy Hotel, I found myself sharing an elevator with Richard, who was walking a dog with an elegant collar. When I smiled, he scrutinized me quizzically.

"I know that you know me, and most espe-cially do I know that you know me," he said, his delivery making it sound like a song lyric.

"In no way do I want to interfere with your thought process," I said as the elevator doors opened.

In my memories, Swingin' London has a beautiful rhythm, and the city itself soars like an unforgettable symphony. I've been lucky in vocation and location. I was in New York for the 1930s, California for the 1940s, and thereafter often moved back and forth between the coasts. I was in the Sunbelt from the mid-1970s on. And for a glorious period, I was in Swingin' London. Who could ask for more?

10

Gary Cooper

~

Ever since the early 1940s, I had wanted to go into production. I felt my gifts as a catalyst for talented, creative people would be of greatest use in producing a film. Besides, the idea of being a producer appealed to me. And, with my first production, 1959's *The Hanging Tree*, the reality of being a producer was as terrific as I thought it would be.

Both financially and artistically, I felt fortified to begin production. For years Hal Wallis and his partner Joseph Hazen had been telling me that I should be a producer and that they would help me in any way they could.

Eagerly, and for the moment blissfully forgetting that Wallis was one of the most tight-fisted men in Hollywood, I met with them at their office. They were pleasant. They listened. They smiled. They nodded. And they did nothing more. They wished me luck but offered no financial backing to ensure that luck would come my way. As is often the case in Hollywood, word is spoken but not executed.

I thought back. I had brought into Hal's fold such talent as Burt Lancaster, Elvis Presley, Kirk Douglas, Dean Martin, and Jerry Lewis. I had encouraged him to put Shirley MacLaine under contract. But Hal felt he had repaid me with experience. Under his tutelage, he thought I had learned lessons that no other master could teach.

From his perspective, he probably was right. I've always considered him a truly great producer. But from my perspective, I desperately needed financing. It was a painful moment when I went home to tell Erin-Jo that no funds were forthcoming. As always, she offered encouragement and support.

I was friends with a young, effective agent named Richard Shepherd, who also longed to go into production. He was the son-in-law of William Goetz, for many years a powerful force at 20th Century Fox and the producer of such prestigious films as 1943's *The Song of Bernadette*. Besides which, Mr. Goetz was the son-in-law of Louis B.

GARY COOPER

Mayer, whose legendary stature had actually increased since his death in 1957.

And so, late in 1958, Dick Shepherd and I met with Mr. Goetz, who had enjoyed an enormous success the previous year with *Sayonara*. With Bill Goetz, there was no game-playing.

"How much do you need to get started?" he asked.

"Fifty thousand dollars," we answered.

"This is Friday. The money will be in your bank account, at your disposal, on Tuesday morning," he said. "I trust you to pay me back as soon as possible."

He was as good as his word. And I paid him back as soon as I could, from my initial payments for producing *The Hanging Tree*. Our first production, *The Hanging Tree* was a success. And it starred a giant among men, the majestic Gary Cooper.

It was appropriate that my first personal production should be a western. They're the most American of any film genre, and I've always revered them. As a youngster, I couldn't wait to see the newest Tom Mix oater. Earlier in 1958, I had liked the novelette *The Hanging Tree* by Dorothy M. Johnson, who hailed from the same part of Montana as Gary Cooper. Not a conventional shoot-'em-up, it told a strong and probing story, and the role of Doc Frail, a man striving to overcome a personal tragedy, would be one of the finest of Cooper's autumnal years.

Our sponsor Bill Goetz was a good friend of Coop and arranged for us to meet with him. Coop had read the initial script and indicated interest. When Dick and I met him at his Montana ranch, he was sleepy. He invited us to join him in a cabin away from the main house, where he said he liked to read and relax.

Cooper was a tall man, seeming even taller than his six feet four inches. Instead of using his height as an advantage, he sought to make us physical equals. Once inside the cabin, he sank into what he said was his favorite chair. The chair that he extended to me actually made me rise in height. Thanks to Gary's gallantry, we were indeed equals in physical stature.

As we talked about *The Hanging Tree*'s unusual storyline and psychological symbolism, Coop nodded, closed his eyes and seemed to fall asleep. But my instinct told me he had closed his eyes in concentration and that his consciousness was absorbing every word Dick and I uttered.

As I watched this pillar of cinematic strength sitting quietly in his favorite chair, a parade of movie titles marched through my mind: *Mr. Deeds Goes to Town* and *The Lives of a Bengal Lancer* in the 1930s, *Sergeant York* and *Pride of the Yankees* in the 1940s, *High Noon* and *Friendly Persuasion* in the 1950s. With only half these titles, Coop would have been a major star. With all of them, he was a legend.

He seemed like a shy and gentle man, but he was known as a man of action with women. Early in his career, in the late 1920s, he was linked with "It Girl" Clara Bow. The international society queen Countess Dorothy di Frasso gave him a make-over from Montana cowboy to 1930s bon vivant. Early in that decade, he was an object of lust for the fireball Lupe Velez. And in the 1940s, he was drawn to the ravishing Ingrid Bergman, and, most dramatically in the 1950s, to the sophisticated, aristocratic Patricia Neal.

Some felt that Coop's Park Avenue wife Rocky was aloof, particularly in contrast to her husband's quiet warmth. But Rocky actually was a

A rare photo of Gary Cooper—a star who earned the label of gentleman—taken during the making of *The Hanging Tree* in 1959.

65

shy woman. Shyness is a quality not often found in Hollywood circles, and it's sometimes misinterpreted as coldness.

After we finished expounding on the virtues of *The Hanging Tree*, Gary opened his eyes and said slowly, "Sounds good. Sounds really good."

By the end of the 1950s, Cooper needed a hit almost as much as we wanted one. He was rebounding from several films that had not done the business expected from a Gary Cooper venture. He was miscast both as a playboy in Billy Wilder's 1957 comedy *Love in the Afternoon* with Audrey Hepburn and as a weary tycoon in 1958's *Ten North Frederick*. He had hoped that a return to the frontier with *Man of the West* would stop the downward slide. But a hip injury prevented him from being as physically graceful as was his wont, and his discomfort was obvious. *Man of the West*, released in 1957, became the most painful of his recent disappointments.

But *The Hanging Tree*'s emphasis was on characterization. Relatively little riding was required, which soothed Coop's somewhat morose spirits.

Dick and I returned to Hollywood, two very happy first-time producers. We knew the script needed work. And once again Coop had shown his mettle. Unlike most other major stars, he had agreed to do the film without a finished script.

But shortly after Dick and I returned to Warner Bros., our feeling of good fortune headed south. Our screenwriter had to leave for another assignment. Suddenly we were producing without a script.

Then a friendship I made during my studio and agency days paid off richly. Delmer Daves, a wonderful friend and a gifted director/screenwriter

never fully appreciated by film historians, agreed to take over *The Hanging Tree*'s reins.

All started harmoniously. My dear friend Karl Malden played the neurotic villain Frenchy. Maria Schell had been an art-house sensation when playing Emile Zola's tragic Gervaise in 1956, but her American feature debut opposite Yul Brynner in 1958's *The Brothers Karamazov* had not been greeted with enthusiasm. Still, we thought she would be perfect for our unconventional heroine, a temporarily blind woman.

One piece of casting involved a bit of happenstance that makes me gleeful in retrospect. The screenplay contained the part of a fiery preacher with the Dickensian name of Dr. Grubb. But we had finally written the preacher out of the script because we had given up on finding an actor intense enough to play the part.

I was in New York on business and met Jane Dacey, an agent friend. She insisted that I speak with a young client of hers, an actor who she said redefined intensity. Intrigued, I agreed. Later that afternoon, he walked through my office door. I watched his determined, focused stride. It was the walk of a man who doesn't mince words, and I could sense a strong and solid containment in him. This was all I needed.

He began to speak. "My name is . . ."

"George C. Scott," I responded. Even if I hadn't been prompted by Jane, I would have felt that he redefined intensity. I offered him my hand, while grabbing the nearest phone with my other hand. Instantly I called Dick in Los Angeles.

"Put the preacher back in. We've found our preacher. Yes, yes, he's intense enough," I whispered into the receiver, sounding mighty intense myself.

Karl Malden played *The Hanging Tree*'s neurotic villain. But on the set, he was a hero.

I hope this is
the beginning of many
more for you and The
Thank you
Karl Malden

George C. Scott had done only minimal work in the theater at that time. I didn't care. I was sold on his great walk, his piercing eyes. Later he acquired a reputation as a man of short temper. But he worked excellently with us.

For *The Hanging Tree*, we built a mining camp forty miles from Yakima, Washington, and all exteriors were filmed there. Coop was known for eating by himself in his dressing room, not out of snobbery, as some insisted, but out of that sense of solitude and rectitude that was his persona. But on this film, he joined all of us in the chow line and on the lunch benches. He knew he was more easily tired than ever, and he enjoyed the enthusiasm of first-time producers. To him, we seemed to represent the future of the industry he dearly loved. Always the most loyal of friends, he had great confidence in his longtime acting coach Louise Vincent, who was on the set daily to go over his lines and correct his interpretation.

For a while, all went swimmingly. Delmer was an avid rock collector, and he made some great discoveries on the Washington location. Yakima was the source of delicious, juicy Washington State apples, and each day, we would distribute the prized fruit to cast and crew. Coop loved apples and grinned like a little boy.

It was a wonderful learning experience for me. Trying not to interfere with the crew, I nevertheless wanted to learn as much as I could. I spoke with the cameramen and made note of what lenses they used. I talked with editors and watched construction crews at work. I was never away from the set unless business dictated so. And along the way, I established a reputation for sitting on top of the movies I produced.

Sometimes my curiosity got me into serio-comic jams. Delmer was using a new apparatus that allowed someone, while buckled into a small seat, to be moved out into the open spaces to watch an action scene down below. This contraption took me high above a canyon where a horse-riding scene was taking place. In my enthusiasm at getting a view from the top, I forgot that I have a lifelong fear of heights. I couldn't wait to get down.

Just as Delmer, Dick, Coop, and I congratulated ourselves on the ease of the production, everything threatened to collapse. Delmer was rushed to the hospital with an emergency appendectomy. I was fearful for my friend's health, and Dick and I were beside ourselves with concern and panic.

The shooting would have to be shut down for two weeks, costing $400,000 on a $1.6 million budget. The studio panicked. Warner Bros. was in no condition to add $400,000 to a movie's budget. But after our own panic had subsided, and the doctors had announced Delmer's improvement, Dick and I reached a solution that would absolve *The Hanging Tree*'s temporary death sentence.

We were in constant communication with the ever-bombastic studio head Jack Warner.

J. L. was yelling through the phone as only J. L. could, bombarding me with questions and invectives.

Very calmly I took a pleasurable pause and then replied, "Don't worry, J. L. We're already shooting. We have a director and an executive producer."

"Shooting? Who's shooting?" said a furious J. L. "You're shooting a western without a director. Who's shooting what?"

Imagining J. L. turning several different colors

Marty with Maria Schell on the Washington state set of *The Hanging Tree*.
The Austria-born actress had her most successful American role in Marty's first personal production.

at the other end of the line, I continued speaking with confidence and serenity. "The executive producer is Gary Cooper. The director is Karl Malden."

Coop's name obviously had a profound effect on J. L.'s affirmative decision. And naturally the prospect of saving money helped.

At the end of each day, Gary, Karl, Dick, and I would visit Delmer in the hospital. Delmer would sketch out all the shots that he felt necessary for the next day's filming. All of us, including Coop, would take notes. Ever the complete professional, he would hunch over Delmer's bedside, notebook in hand, and write down Delmer's instructions. It was a dream team: Gary, Karl, and Delmer.

The Hanging Tree, finished on schedule and on budget, was a critical and commercial hit. Its Marty Robbins theme song topped the charts, too. Strong music was something I insisted on during all my years in production.

I was exalted that out of the unexpected moments of chaos came a film of unity, solidarity, and strong entertainment values. And I was overjoyed at the opportunity of working with the revered Gary Cooper. This strong and silent man had a genuinely sweet soul.

Coop made only three more films before his death in 1961. The last time I saw him was shortly before he died, when he was being feted at an honorary dinner in Los Angeles. He looked so sweet, so peaceful, so calm, but as we embraced, something about his body English told me he sensed the end was near.

Years later, I was to get the same sensation when I had a final embrace with beloved Audrey Hepburn. At times the human touch can convey more emotions than a thousand words. And create just as many poignant memories.

11

Holly Golightly

~

It was an unforgettable moment, that evening in 1991 when Audrey Hepburn was honored by the USA Film Festival in Dallas.

Audrey and I had not seen each other for years, and we embraced with the fervor of dear friends who were not certain we would meet again.

I had no way of knowing that within two years, this elegant, elfin woman would be gone from us. But when the telephone rang with the tragic news, I thought back to our tender, bittersweet embrace. When Audrey was your friend, there could be no one more loyal or steadfast.

Richard Shepherd and I had the privilege of producing *Breakfast at Tiffany's*, which became her favorite film despite her initial apprehension that its central character Holly Golightly was, in her own deliciously Audrey-like phrase, "a veritable hooker."

But Audrey's and my friendship began a decade earlier, when I was with the William Morris Agency and Audrey was the year's most sparkling newcomer.

The year was 1953, and Audrey was everywhere. The aristocratic gamine was the daughter of a baroness. She already had become a New York name in 1951 when Colette, legendary chronicler of wicked Parisian lifestyles, selected her to star in the stage production of her naughty-but-nice *Gigi*. And in 1953, she was enchanting moviegoers as the runaway princess in *Roman Holiday*, and her farewell to Gregory Peck melted everyone's heart.

Concurrent with *Roman Holiday's* release, she was to star on Broadway in the potentially lovely but difficult-to-mount *Ondine*. Her costar was the handsomely chiseled Mel Ferrer, with whom she was deeply in love and who would become her husband.

The popular concept of the Hepburn/Ferrer marriage was that when Audrey's shining star continued to eclipse Mel's tenuous footing within the Hollywood galaxy, their relationship suffered. But it is far from accurate to depict Audrey as a spotlight-craving superstar with a sensitive spouse. Whenever possible, Audrey deferred to

Mel. She had been trained as a ballerina, and she considered Mel her governing maestro. And when I saw a photo of Mel at Audrey's funeral, twenty-five years after their divorce, his face was filled with grief.

Ondine tested the mettle of all its participants, Audrey in particular. And she passed the test with natural style. In this romantic fable, Audrey wore the flimsiest of costumes. Mel, alas, wore the heaviest of armor. In a display of thoughtfulness rare in major stars, Audrey insisted that Mel occupy the star dressing room on the first floor, while she would be content with the smaller second-floor accommodations.

Ondine was produced by a formidable group called The Playwrights, whose members included Elmer Rice (*Street Scene*) and my dear friend Robert Sherwood (*Idiot's Delight*, *The Petrified Forest*). The play was directed by Alfred Lunt, who had achieved legendary status as an actor, usually teamed with his imperial wife Lynn Fontanne. At least he thought he was director. But by the time *Ondine* reached Boston for try-outs, the regal Alfred was ready to shoot upstart Mel Ferrer. Mel was completely governing Audrey's performance, dictating notes on how it could be improved. Mel's interference threatened to lead to a cancellation of the entire production.

Mr. Sherwood, an important client for William Morris, beckoned me to Boston, where I heard the entire chaotic story and arranged a meeting with Audrey. That meeting was the start of one of the warmest friendships of my life.

She listened to me and then looked at me with her doelike eyes.

"Martin, I'm aware of everything that's been going on," she said. "But I have to tell you to tell them that if Mel goes, I go, too."

Those wonderful eyes turned even more pensive and she added in the sweetest, most self-effacing tones imaginable, "Why not pay a little more attention to Mel?"

At the age of twenty-five, she already was a very wise woman.

I took her helpful words to Mr. Lunt and said, "Try to find something wrong with Mel's armor. Devote yourself not to the performance but to Mel's armor."

Thus, *Ondine* was saved and so was Mel's ego.

In 1961 Truman Capote's *Breakfast at Tiffany's* was one of the most coveted of properties. Its life-loving heroine Holly Golightly would make a wonderful role for the right actress. Truman had based Holly on several women he knew in New York, among them Gloria Vanderbilt and Carol Marcus. Carol was an aspiring actress who would marry William Saroyan and, later, Walter Matthau.

Some important talents, including Joshua Logan, were aware that *Tiffany's* had the making of a cinematic gem. They all had their people call Truman's people. But Dick Shepherd and I were determined to make *Tiffany's* our own. Always believing in going directly to the source, I flew to New York to meet with the imperious author.

Audrey Wood, a wonderful woman and outstanding agent who represented such talents as Tennessee Williams and Truman Capote, arranged for Truman and me to meet at his favorite gathering place, the posh Colony Club.

Only Mae West could have made a bigger production out of entering a room. All eyes were on him, which was exactly how he wanted it. He

Audrey Hepburn, the one-and-only, unforgettable Holly Golightly.

was a pixie, a leprechaun. But a leprechaun with a giant ego.

He was in his element at the Colony, with his own table, his own group of waiters, his own telephone, and his own wine. His eyes were always darting about, taking mental notes of which socialites and celebrities were looking his way. Over the next several hours, I was only able to get in a few words, all of them praising his work and its cinematic potential. Finally I declared Dick's and my desire to make the film and our loyalty to his ideas regarding the story.

My fervor seemed to incite his enthusiasm, but my loyalty to his ideas was about to be sorely tested.

"You know, of course, that I want to play the male lead," he said, tossing off the line in a manner too firm to be dismissed.

I stared. I gulped. Was he testing me? Was he playing games? No, he was absolutely serious. And he definitely thought he would be a logical choice.

I wrestled for a solution that would both stroke his ego and change his mind.

"Truman, the role just isn't good enough for you," I said, recalling his delight when all eyes followed his grand entrance. "All eyes will be on Holly Golightly through every frame of the picture. The male lead is just a pair of shoulders for Holly to lean on. You deserve something more dynamic, more colorful."

He paused for an interminable moment. Then he said, "You're right. I deserve something more dynamic."

We met the next day in Audrey Wood's office. I felt certain that if I spoke the right words, the deal would be closed. I knew that Truman needed money to continue his lordly style of living, which included decorating his home in the Hamptons. When we closed the deal for $50,000, lights

were shining in his eyes. Then I did something that granted me Truman's complete appreciation, however temporary that proved to be.

"Is this a deal, Truman?" I asked

"Yes, it is," he replied eagerly.

"Then I'm going to give Truman another $15,000," I announced, raising the purchase price to a then-princely $65,000. Later I heard that Truman was unhappy that he hadn't received a percentage of the film's profits, which probably contributed to his bitterness. Actually, I pleaded with Paramount to give him points, but the moguls didn't want to give a mere writer such preferential treatment.

On the plane back to Los Angeles, I looked to my left and discovered Marilyn Monroe sitting next to me. Marilyn was vibrant when excited but vague and disoriented at practically all other times.

She had been in New York and knew about *Breakfast at Tiffany's* from Milton Greene, a photographer who vied with Lee Strasberg's wife Paula to rank as Marilyn's top advisor. She had not read the book, but she had heard about the character of Holly Golightly from her "feeders"—people like Milton and Paula.

When I told her that Dick Shepherd and I had the rights to Capote's novella, her immediate reaction was, "This is a plot! First, Milton Greene tells me about this Holly Golightly person! And now you're sitting next to me! This is a plot!"

I assured her that no such conspiracy had been planned. Although some of her people were interested in the project, I felt that casting Marilyn as Holly would be too obvious. Yet, for an instant, she truly seemed like Holly Golightly. In the film, the Hollywood agent played by Martin Balsam says of Holly, "She's a phony. But a real phony." That same phrase could describe Marilyn.

By the time the plane landed, Marilyn had

had several more drinks and had slipped into her vague and disoriented mode. As we said goodbye, I wasn't sure if she even knew what *Breakfast at Tiffany's* was or who Holly Golightly was.

I was glad that I had said neither yes nor no to Marilyn, but I felt that her enthusiasm would be good for the project.

Within two days, I received a call from Paula Strasberg, Marilyn's fearless and intimidating coach. Marilyn had discussed *Tiffany's* with Paula.

"There is no way she will play that girl," said Paula, with all the force you would expect of Lee Strasberg's wife. "Marilyn Monroe will not play a call girl, a lady of the evening."

Still, that wasn't the last I heard about Marilyn as Holly. I'm still not sure if Truman ever really forgave me for not casting him in the male lead. When he first saw our movie, he professed to love the film and Audrey's interpretation. But later he made unkind criticisms of Audrey's sparkling performance, saying that Marilyn Monroe would have been better in the part.

Meanwhile, there were other candidates. Shirley MacLaine was interested, but she was committed to MGM for *Two Loves*, which unfortunately would bomb. In that film, Shirley was very non-Golightly in the role of a spinster schoolteacher, but her remarkable versatility would serve us all beautifully twenty-two years later in *Terms of Endearment*.

Erin-Jo was very enthusiastic about Jane Fonda, but Dick Shepherd had known Jane while she was growing up and had difficulty seeing her as anything but a sprightly adolescent. And someone at Paramount was convinced that Rosemary Clooney had the perfect zing and gusto for Holly.

Even before Ms. Strasberg's dire speech, Dick and I had never visualized Holly as a call girl. She

was a woman who defied definition. She hated hypocrisy and maintained a live-and-let-live standard for herself and others. While she used sex, she was not sexual.

The actress who seemed most virginally honest for this uniquely irresistible character? Audrey Hepburn.

But getting Audrey was not as easy as making a phone call and saying, "Audrey, dear, I have a script I'd like you to read."

Audrey's agent was Kurt Frings, a ferocious ex-boxer who also represented Elizabeth Taylor. His mind was set. A familiar refrain: his client was not going to play a call girl. I set in motion a series of calls—pleading, begging, coaxing, cajoling the ex-boxer to at least allow me to head for Audrey's home in the south of France, where she was pregnant with her son Sean, and show her the screenplay. He finally relented.

When I met Paramount chieftains Y. Frank Freeman and Barney Balaban at Dinty Moore's in New York and told them my plans, they replied in unison: "No chance."

Audrey, it seems, had just turned down a role in a prospective Alfred Hitchcock thriller, *The Hanging Judge*, because the character was a prostitute. Hardly anyone had the courage to refuse Hitch, but Audrey did. What's more, Kurt Frings had a list of directors, people with names like Wyler, Wilder, Cukor, and Mankiewicz, whom he considered the only possible candidates to guide Audrey on-screen. Dick and I had seen the Cary Grant service comedy *Operation Petticoat*. Impressed with its spirited pace, we felt its director Blake Edwards should be at the *Tiffany's* helm. Nevertheless, our hearts belonged to Audrey.

"I'll tell you what I'm going to do," I told the Paramount honchos at Dinty Moore's. "I'm going to do what Hitch did not do. I'm going to get off

Blake Edwards, Audrey Hepburn, and Audrey's Yorkshire terrier. On-screen, Holly Golightly's pet was the nameless Cat, but off-screen, Audrey was crazy about her Yorkie.

this chair. And I'm going to fly to Audrey in the south of France."

And so I did, to be greeted with the warmth and forthrightness of our *Ondine* meeting almost a decade earlier.

"Oh, Martin, you have a wonderful script," said Audrey, who was not the type to use the shorter, more colloquial "Marty."

And then she said, as only Audrey could: "But I cannot play a veritable hooker."

That was the turning point. I rose to my full height and declared, with the righteous indignation of Henry Higgins confronting Eliza Dolittle. "I cannot believe you don't know the difference between a hooker and a dreamer of dreams, a lopsided romantic. If you think we want to make a

The house where Holly Golightly lived on East 71st Street, Manhattan's East Side, painted by the famous watercolorist Dong Kingman.

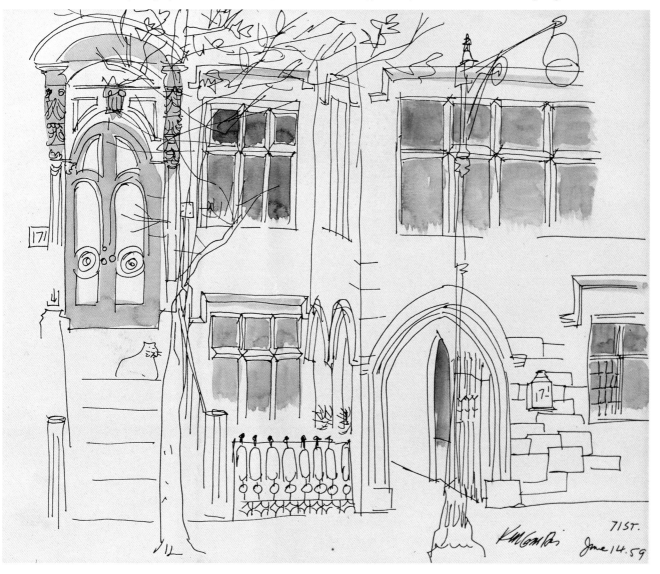

movie about a veritable hooker, we don't want you near the script!"

Suddenly tears were flowing down those magnificent, exquisite cheekbones. In the same sweet tones she had used when pleading Mel's case in *Ondine*, she said, "Oh, Martin, Martin, it will be all right."

And, of course, it was much more than merely all right.

The filming of *Breakfast at Tiffany's* provided a

William Holden (far left) visits the set of *Breakfast at Tiffany's*. Producer Marty (left foreground) confers with director Blake Edwards.

feast of wonderful memories. Audrey was the consummate professional. She wasn't interested in the film from merely her own perspective. She was intrigued by all aspects of filmmaking. She contributed great ideas about Holly's wardrobe and accessories, not in the slyly grande dame manner

of Loretta Young but as a genuine help to the production.

She sought Givenchy to design her clothes, and he created a stunning wardrobe, including a tuxedo shirt that was titillating for 1961. And it was Audrey's idea to have streaks in her hair.

Blake and Audrey got along instantly. And for Blake and me, it was the beginning of a warm and productive association. Blake would be important to the careers of two "fair ladies"—Audrey and Julie Andrews, whom he would marry.

Although hardly a prude—she loved hearing all the latest gossip—Audrey was not a sexually driven woman. And her air of innocence was perfect for our interpretation of Holly Golightly. She was still with Mel, who seemed more bitter than ever, often making critical remarks about his wife.

But Audrey knew how to handle him, as she handled most people, with decorum and diplomacy. Certainly both she and Patricia Neal, who played a Manhattan socialite, handled George Peppard deftly. George arrived on the set fully convinced of his star potential and felt that his character was the real center of attention. He was disappointed when Audrey didn't respond to him on a personal level and referred to her as "The Happy Nun."

For many of us, *Breakfast at Tiffany's* brought good fortune. Pat Neal, who had endured a roller-coaster career, was delighted to be playing a glamorous part with luxurious wardrobes and settings. Two years later she would win the Oscar for her hard-bitten housekeeper in *Hud*. And that would begin yet another chapter in her courageous life.

I had known Buddy Ebsen well in my MCA days. His portrayal of Holly's forsaken rural husband was flawless and heart-wrenching. He was so convincing in the role that *The Beverly Hillbillies* was only a short time away.

George Peppard (left) with Blake Edwards on the *Breakfast at Tiffany's* set. George would never admit it, but his role was to provide Holly with a calm shoulder.

We caught some criticism for casting Mickey Rooney as Holly's frantic Japanese neighbor. But Mickey always made me laugh, and the film did great in Japan, where audiences loved his performance.

Breakfast at Tiffany's did run into trouble with the censors. But not for any expected reasons. They wanted us to cut the scene in which Audrey and Peppard steal Halloween masks from a five-and-dime. They felt that as a result of this scene, youngsters all across America would rob neighborhood dime stores. The scene remained, and I seriously doubt it added to delinquent crime.

The film contains at least two scenes that remain indelible in moviegoers' minds. In one, Audrey sits on a fire escape, her face the epitome of poignancy, and sings Henry Mancini's "Moon River" in the most halting yet tender voice imaginable. In another lovely moment, Audrey eats a breakfast roll while silently, wistfully gazing into Tiffany's show windows.

The film's sneak preview in San Francisco was a shining success. But Paramount brass wanted to cut the scene of Audrey singing on the fire escape.

"She can't carry a tune!" was their unanimous chorus.

Blake left the room in a huff. I stayed and argued. And argued and argued. I felt that Audrey sang "Moon River" exactly as Holly would have sung it.

The song remained in the film and became a classic. Blake had worked with Henry Mancini on the television series *Peter Gunn* and wisely wanted

(Left to right) Composer Henry Mancini, lyricist Johnny Mercer, and Marty were all the best of "huckleberry friends."

to use him for the movie. Henry's entire score was a triumph. When I first heard the phrase "huckleberry friend" from "Moon River," I knew we had struck gold. I urged Paramount to make Henry Mancini a high-profile name with the general public. They were initially hesitant. Why treat a mere composer as if he were a celebrity? Eventually they did promotions on him, and he became a household name.

But what would *Breakfast at Tiffany's* have been without an actual Tiffany's?

It took six months of cajoling before Tiffany's honcho Walter Hoving granted permission for us to film inside the Fifth Avenue landmark. He agreed only after considerable nudging from Letitia Baldridge, the public relations maven who at the time handled PR for the firm. Letitia soon would become the White House social secretary during the Kennedy years.

Mr. Hoving would graciously say that the store's expansion was largely due to the movie. But at the time, without telling me, he canceled the company's insurance on the Saturday of our filming. Lloyds of London's New York office was closed, so I spent the day on the phone, frantically trying to get hold of the Lloyds' home office in London before we began shooting. Happily, I was successful, and we got the insurance.

When Erin-Jo and I last saw Audrey in Dallas, she was radiant. At the film festival's gala, many women came up to Audrey, Erin-Jo, and myself to tell us how *Breakfast at Tiffany's* had encouraged them to forge their own paths in the big city. That was always the case with the film, and its reputation grows with each year.

Audrey's reputation also has grown with each year. In 1999, the American Film Institute polled film scholars and filmmakers to name the screen's fifty most legendary actresses. Audrey placed third, behind Katharine Hepburn and Bette Davis. Her impact on cinema, fashion, and simple human decency will continue long after her death.

Always a lover of children, she had become a revered emissary for UNICEF. And she had found a wonderful companion in Robert Wolders, the handsome widower of Merle Oberon. She was Robert's partner, lover, and child all rolled into one.

When I saw television coverage of Audrey's funeral and watched a bereft Mel embrace Robert, I was deeply moved. And I recalled one of the dearest sounds in the world—the timbre of Audrey's sweet voice saying "Oh, Martin, Martin, it will be all right."

At heart, this most aristocratic of actresses really was a "huckleberry friend."

12

The Passion of Anna Magnani

~

My life in show business often plays like a cavalcade of anecdotes, flavored by rich, stormy passions. Any mention of passion recalls the Italian dynamo Anna Magnani, an illustrious woman of fiery temperament.

I represented her at the William Morris Agency in the 1950s and produced *The Fugitive Kind* in 1959, which teamed her with Marlon Brando. With her penetrating eyes and savagely beautiful face, she was a commanding presence both on and off the screen. She always said exactly what she thought, yet never purposely set out to insult anyone.

Anna became earth mother of the international post-World War II movie scene with her shattering, earthy performance in Roberto Rossellini's neo-realistic classic *Roma: Open City.*

Her luminous humanity and aggressive sexuality were apparent in every frame of Rossellini's stunning film. They also were apparent in every frame of Rossellini's private life. Anna and Roberto were with each other constantly—loving and fighting, but, at least in Anna's mind, mostly loving.

And then Ingrid Bergman entered Rossellini's life, and for all three of them, nothing was ever the same again. Ingrid and Roberto pursued each other, leaving Anna right where someone of her incendiary nature hated to be—out in the cold. To the end of her life, Anna constantly rekindled her hatred of Ingrid.

It wasn't simply that Anna felt Ingrid had stolen Roberto from her. Anna never forgave Ingrid for deserting her daughter, who became the television personality Pia Lindstrom. Ingrid later felt considerable remorse over the pain she caused Pia. But for Anna, who constantly grieved over her own polio-stricken son, that wasn't enough. To Anna, children were sacred.

Anna loved her family dearly, but her personal life was always in shambles. No matter how good her intentions, she did not possess the kind of personality that nurtures a stable family life. She envied Ingrid's ability to enjoy herself. For all the

Anna Magnani was tempestuous, temperamental, and terrific, both as an actress and as a woman.
How could any man reject her? (Photo taken on the set of *The Fugitive Kind*, 1959.)

trauma of Ingrid's life, she knew how to create happiness for herself and others. With Anna, happiness always alternated with despair. If Ingrid resembled a dulcet stream, Anna had the emotional rush of a raging river.

Tennessee Williams wrote *The Rose Tattoo* for

Anna. But her limited command of English made her hesitant to do the play, and Maureen Stapleton, also to be featured in *The Fugitive Kind*, played the passionate widow Serafina on Broadway. But when Hal Wallis made the 1955 movie version, Anna played the part and took the public by storm. She

In 1959 few movies were as eagerly awaited as *The Fugitive Kind*, in its premiere at the Astor Theater on Times Square.
With a cast like this, what could go wrong? (Photo by Kas Heppner, Metropolitan Photo Service, Inc., NYC)

won the Oscar, in a tight race with *I'll Cry Tomorrow*'s Susan Hayward, but she stayed in Rome and did not attend the ceremonies.

The next year, however, she attended in full regalia to present the 1956 best actor Oscar to Yul Brynner for *The King and I*. She received a tremendous ovation, wearing a sparkling gown that seemed to say, "Hello, Hollywood! Here I am!"

And yet even on that triumphant evening, I couldn't help feeling that Ingrid, unintentionally, was a thorn amidst Anna's glitter. That was the year of Ingrid's comeback in *Anastasia*. Although not present to receive her Academy Award, Ingrid was at the center of all the Oscar buzz. This must have reopened wounds that, for Anna, would never completely heal.

And what memories that Oscar night stirred for me! It was a triumph for both Anna and Ingrid, two women I admired both personally and professionally. And Yul won for *The King and I*, which almost hadn't opened on Broadway.

But those memories pale alongside another evening in which the magnificent Magnani played a starring role.

A year later, Anna would return to Hollywood to film *Wild Is the Wind* for Wallis. And wild was Anna after she took one look at Anthony Franciosa, her much younger costar.

Anna was not overly concerned that Tony Franciosa was a newlywed, and that his bride happened to be Shelley Winters. When it was slyly suggested to Anna that Shelley was no weakling, she simply shrugged and muttered something in Italian.

But Shelley's antenna was up, and she was soon aware that late-night rehearsals between Anna and Tony were getting more frequent.

Then came the night I received a call from Anna. With only the slightest hint of urgency, she suggested that it might be wise if I came to her hotel suite at the Chateau Mormant in Hollywood. "Might be wise"! That was the only time I knew Anna to make an understatement.

I didn't know what to expect, but I sensed it was going to be one dramatic evening. When I got to the legendary vintage hotel, I was greeted by a scene as stormy as any recorded on film.

Shelley and Anna were circling each other like Roman gladiators. Suddenly Shelley's anger was directed more at me than at her rival in romance. Since I was Anna's agent, Shelley felt that I was the procurer, that I had arranged for Tony to satisfy the sexual needs of my client.

Suddenly I realized that one participant in this affair was nowhere to be seen.

"Where's Tony?" I asked.

"He's in the bathroom!" screamed Shelley, her eyes livid. "He's locked the door, and he's not coming out! And if you know what's good for the movie and good for your client, you'll put an immediate stop to what's going on. Or I'll pull Tony from the movie."

My protests of innocence fell on silent ears. Shelley got increasingly angry, and her eyes focused on a large knife that rested on the kitchen table. In one swift lightning stroke, Shelley went for the knife and approached me in the dining room, her body shaking with fury.

During this time, I hoarsely shouted for Tony, who remained behind locked bathroom doors.

Anna, standing in the kitchen, smashed a half-empty bottle of Paisano in the sink. As Shelley approached me, Anna approached Shelley, thrusting the bottle's jagged edge toward her.

Still no Tony.

But the ultimate threat of violence came from Anna. "You kill Martin, I kill you!" she screamed at Shelley in true take-no-prisoners fashion.

Shelley suddenly changed her tactics. Her face

blanched, she delicately placed her knife back on the kitchen table and started to walk out of the room.

With a studied combination of nonchalance and scorn, Shelley said, "You can have him. I don't want him."

Not to be outdone, Anna shouted back in a voice that must have echoed through the Hollywood Hills. "I send him back to you! Do you hear, I send him back to you!"

And then Anna wickedly added, "Just one more rehearsal. That's all. Just one more rehearsal, then I send him back."

The evening that had started as a Gothic horror show had ended as a bedroom farce. Exhausted, I regained as much of my dignity as I

could and called Erin-Jo from the hotel lobby. Could she possibly come pick me up? Somehow I was too tired to drive.

Still, I wonder how many men can claim that their life was saved by Anna Magnani? Not only saved, but enriched.

She was at heart a dear creature, with a penchant for excess. Prior to the 1959 shooting of *The Fugitive Kind*, I met with Anna and her attorney in Rome. I admired the work of the painter Severini that decorated the attorney's offices. I was at the airport, leaving for Los Angeles, when a courier arrived delivering one of the paintings, a goodwill gift from the attorney. When Anna arrived in Los Angeles a few weeks later, she brought a Vespignani painting for me and a vicuna throw-blanket

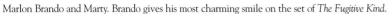

Marlon Brando and Marty. Brando gives his most charming smile on the set of *The Fugitive Kind*.

The ever-manipulative Marlon tries to work his charm on Erin-Jo as she cuts Sidney's cake. Sidney's at the far left.

for Erin-Jo. She wasn't in competition with her attorney. She was simply capable of enormous warmth and generosity. Anna resembled a mythical goddess, whose love and loyalty were greater than those of mere mortals.

With *The Fugitive Kind*, everything looked perfect on paper. Dick Shepherd and I assembled an incomparably strong cast headed by Marlon Brando, Anna Magnani, Joanne Woodward, and Maureen Stapleton. Our talented young director

Sidney Lumet blows out his birthday candles on the set of *The Fugitive Kind*. At left, Richard Shepherd and Marty; Marlon Brando at the right.

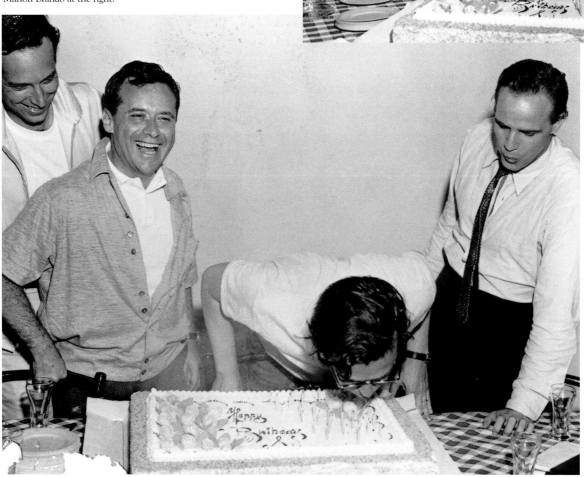

was Sidney Lumet, whose earlier credits included the memorable *12 Angry Men* and who later would bring us *The Pawnbroker*, *Serpico*, and *Dog Day Afternoon*. And, of course, a screenplay based on *Orpheus Descending*, by the sweet, tormented genius Tennessee Williams. What could possibly go wrong?

Just about everything.

And yet, despite the dent that the production made in my personal finances, I look back on the whole enterprise with enormous fondness. I wish the film had been a hit, but I've never regretted making it. I'm truly fond of the movie, and it's a treasure trove of memories. Cracked as this piece of my mosaic is, I wouldn't trade it for anything.

As she had done with *The Rose Tattoo*, Maureen Stapleton created the lead role on Broadway. In our film version, Maureen would play an important supporting role as the sheriff's sad wife, while Anna would play lonely, lusty Lady Torrance.

Maureen, a lovable, outspoken woman as well as a superb actress, shrugged her shoulders and said, "What the hell, the part's good, and the paycheck's good." Erin-Jo and I today enjoy a sweet friendship with her.

I had spoken with Anna when I decided to make the leap into personal production. She told me that she would love to star in a movie version of Tennessee's *Orpheus Descending*, and we pledged to make the film together.

Director Sidney Lumet (left) and cinematographer Boris Levin on the set of *The Fugitive Kind*.
Sidney's probably thinking, "Thank God it's New York and not Hollywood!"

Maureen Stapleton on the set of *The Fugitive Kind*, 1959. She provided a safety net if Anna Magnani proved too difficult.

Joanne Woodward, happily married to Paul Newman, was amused and even startled by the antics of her costars
in *The Fugitive Kind*. Here she's wearing her own Fortuny dress . . . pack and go, no wrinkles. (Fortuny was a Venetian fabric
fancied by the fashion elite in the '40s, '50s, and '60s, and is highly collectible today.)

Marty on the deserted set of *The Fugitive Kind*, a lull in the shooting. The set was one of the early works of the great production designer Richard Sylbert.

Anna was cast first and for a while, Dick and I thought of Anthony Franciosa as the wandering Val Xavier. Val arrives in a small Southern town, wearing a tight snakeskin jacket, and ignites the passions of Anna's Lady Torrance and Joanne Woodward's Carol Cutrere, a free-living young woman estranged from her proud Southern family.

Tony could strut around persuasively in Val's snakeskin jacket, but we wondered if he could register the character's smoldering qualities. And memories of that wild Chateau Mormant night with Anna, Tony, and Shelley still lingered in my mind.

Despite her dismissive remark to the enraged Shelley—"I only need one more rehearsal, then I send him back to you!"—Anna and Tony frequently enjoyed each other's company. But would their off-screen electricity transfer to the big screen? *Wild Is the Wind* had proved a disappointing follow-up to *The Rose Tattoo*.

But then something happened that changed the casting chemistry of *The Fugitive Kind*: we lured Marlon Brando.

At that time, Marlon was embroiled in a turbulent, costly divorce from Anna Kashfi, mother of his ill-fated son Christian. According to gossip, he currently lacked funds to pay for the divorce. He needed money, he was available, he was perfect for the part.

And the mere thought of occupying the same set as Marlon had Anna glowing in ecstatic anticipation.

"We will make history before the cameras and we will make history at night, too!" she told me.

Anna had it all arranged in her heart and mind. Despite the fact that she had watched Rossellini leave her for Ingrid, it never occurred to Anna that her amorous life would not go as she wished. But, then, she had never dealt with Marlon.

The film was to be released through United Artists, and the UA honchos told me to do everything possible to get Brando. As I remember, studio executive Arthur Krim's words were, "The public will pay to see that guy read the telephone directory!"

Dick and I met with Marlon at his mountainside Mulholland Drive home, the scene of much later sadness with children Christian and Cheyenne. Actually, we met outside his Japanese-styled home. Marlon was having his yard fertilized, and the stench was unmistakable. He couldn't have been more cordial, but he definitely enjoyed seeing our bodies squirm as our nostrils flared.

Despite his admiration for Tennessee, he didn't agree immediately to do *The Fugitive Kind*. He had a complex relationship with the playwright, thinking Tennessee couldn't see him as anyone beyond *A Streetcar Named Desire*'s Stanley Kowalski.

As we waded through the necessary preliminaries, we were overcome with the smell of fertilizer, and our host was the epitome of charm. He was also mischievous and manipulative. And then I quietly spoke words that got his undivided intention.

"Marlon, we will pay you enough to secure your divorce from Anna Kashfi."

In Marlon's case, "enough" meant one million dollars for six weeks' work. This was the first time an actor had been paid such an amount.

United Artists was thrilled that Marlon would be the one to wear the snakeskin jacket. They okayed the salary, but with an amendment that I've always regretted accepting. They asked that I pledge future profits against any possible loss on the movie. I couldn't foresee any losses. The moviegoing public was embracing Tennessee Williams, and our cast was great. I never should have agreed to it, but I was a young, confident producer whose vocabulary did not include "failure."

Meanwhile, Anna and Marlon had not even met, but her personal and professional joy knew no bounds. Then came the first day of rehearsal, an occasion I shall never forget.

Although Anna didn't favor high fashion, she arrived that day in a sparkling, sequined, beaded gown, sporting perfume that was even stronger than Marlon's fertilizer had been. She entered the room like a queen, fully expecting a responsive and loyal consort.

And then Marlon strutted in, wearing the snakeskin jacket that was the symbol of Val Xavier.

Anna was about to make her move.

I pleaded with her, "Let Marlon approach you. Don't do anything yet."

She nodded as if agreeing with me. But I soon realized that she could contain herself no longer.

"Don't, Anna, don't!" I implored.

"I must! I must!" she insisted.

She rushed up to Marlon and exclaimed, "Oh, Marlon, Marlon! Mi amore! Mi amore!"

And Marlon replied, "Oh, Anna, Anna! Mi tante! Mi tante!" My aunt! My aunt!

At that moment, I realized that all was lost.

Anna had been rejected and humiliated, with

Paul Newman and Joanne Woodward, on the set of
The Fugitive Kind, always in step with each other.

Marlon's pointed reference to the difference in their ages. Her face turned rigid as she walked away. And Marlon, with studied nonchalance, walked in the opposite direction.

Marlon took particular pleasure in bringing a succession of young Oriental beauties to his dressing room. I asked him to curtail his beautiful-young-girls routine. But Marlon was no fool and knew how much the studio wanted him. He smiled, put his arm around me and said, "You really drew the short straw on this one, Marty."

A short straw, yes, but a wildly colorful one.

Professionally, Anna and Marlon also had a lack of harmony. Anna came on the set completely prepared and required very few takes. Marlon preferred multiple takes. He either didn't know his lines or else wanted extra time to explore his character. A sense of lethargy, born of Anna's personal frustration and their own disparate acting techniques, set in, and I'm afraid it showed on-screen. Sidney Lumet, then a young director, was not yet experienced enough to handle such volatile emotional cargo as Brando and Magnani.

In contrast to the Marlon/Anna antics was the genuine love and respect shared by Joanne Woodward and Paul Newman. Joanne was both amused and somewhat startled by the actions of her costars, which had become open knowledge on the set. She knew it was a difficult shoot and did everything possible to make things run smoothly.

A smart, intuitive man, Paul respected Marlon as an actor but did not trust him as his wife's costar. Certain that Marlon would make a play for Joanne, Paul came to visit her. Here were Marlon Brando and Paul Newman under the same roof! The traffic around the set was enormous, and

Marty with Paul Newman and Joanne Woodward, worrying about traffic on the set of *The Fugitive Kind*, filmed in Milford, New York.

at one point Paul actually played traffic cop. Those who came to gawk were amazed to see a pleasant Paul Newman telling them which way to turn.

The handsome Newman was surprised and maybe just a little impressed with the effect he had. But he and Joanne always sought privacy, and their mutual respect was obvious. Paul also made creative contributions. He loved to analyze characters, and his suggestions were sensitive and useful.

Marlon treated Paul as a complete equal. And, frankly, Paul was not yet a Brando equal. His greatest performances were in the future. A master manipulator, Marlon wanted Paul to detour the traffic flow from the set. And he knew that Paul would more readily accept the responsibility if the request came from someone who treated him as an equal rather than an inferior.

On the set, Marlon was grace personified. He treated everyone well, all the while treating himself better than anyone. Our relationship was cordial, and we dined together both on the set and at Chinese restaurants.

Marlon was a great flatterer, and he liked to hear himself saying beautiful things to people. He also loved to hear himself addressing significant issues. When he champions worthwhile causes, such as the rights of the Native Americans, I never doubt his earnestness. But I ponder the depth of his sincerity. Marlon could be great company, but sincerity was not his forte. Now that he has witnessed the tragic lives of his children, I understand that he has mellowed, becoming more genuine in his concern for others.

Of course, his pointed preference for younger women made Anna all the more careful about her appearance, and she worried about lines around her throat. One day, I went to Manhattan for a business transaction. When I returned, the set was

Paul Newman photographs his wife, Joanne Woodward, on the set of *The Fugitive Kind*.

closed down. Everyone was gone except for the security guard, who told me Anna had closed the set and that I had better see the makeup man.

When I sought out the heavily burdened makeup man, he told me that Anna had been obsessing about those throat lines and told him that she had read that Marlene Dietrich used a clamp to erase lines. What she really wanted was a certain type of gauze that tightened throat lines, but the poor man had no idea what she meant. After conferring with the crew, he returned with a gigantic clamp borrowed from a gaffer.

Anna was incensed and stormed off the set, causing production to shut down.

Solemnly I went to her dressing quarters. Even more solemnly, I informed her that Maureen knew the part of Lady Torrance perfectly and would be happy to play it on-screen.

"Pack your bags, Anna," I said. "I'm firing you."

"You would fire me?" she said, her face flooded with emotion. "You would not live up to our pledge to make this film together?"

In an instant, we were embracing, everything forgiven. She then demanded that the makeup man be punished for his indiscretion.

"He shall be punished," I stated. "His punishment will be that he may never look at you. Whenever you are in the same area, he is to turn his back."

"Oh, Martin, Martin! That is the perfect punishment for what he did to me. He may never look at my face again."

When I told him of the situation, he said it would be a blessing to turn his back whenever he saw her.

When *The Fugitive Kind* was released, it received some solid notices and in the ensuing years became what is enigmatically known as a "cult film." But it was a loser for the studio. According to our agreement, much of the profit I made from *The Pink Panther* went back to the studio to remove losses on *The Fugitive Kind*.

Following the smash movies of *Cat on a Hot Tin Roof* and *Suddenly, Last Summer*, I may have been wrong in my assumption that the film's timing couldn't be luckier. The public indicated it was suffering from Tennessee Williams overload.

Tennessee occasionally appeared on the set and watched dailies, making encouraging comments. In my Dallas home, I have framed a letter he wrote me after the whole *Fugitive* enterprise.

"I want to tell you personally how much I appreciate the taste and perception, both to a rare degree, that you have shown in your approach to this script," Tennessee wrote. "I have never before worked with a film producer who had these qualities to such a degree."

My career goal had been to become a producer of significant films. Receiving a letter like that from the greatest American playwright is the greatest profit of all.

13

Ava, Sophia, and the Pink Panther

~

Producing *The Pink Panther* was a wonderful experience, populated by shining stars like Peter Sellers, David Niven, Robert Wagner, Ava Gardner, and Sophia Loren.

Ava Gardner and Sophia Loren? The names of these voluptuous women are nowhere on the film's credits. I don't even know how they feel about the film—although I can imagine what thoughts might have filtered through Ava's mind.

Ava's and Sophia's roles as *Pink Panther* muses occurred behind the scenes, but the results of their participation are gloriously apparent in the movie.

Anyone who went to the movies in the 1950s has at least one memorable image of Ava Gardner. Possibly it's of her blowing a kiss to the departing Cotton Blossom in 1951's *Show Boat*. Or of her rendezvous with Gregory Peck in a Paris bistro in 1952's *The Snows of Kilimanjaro*. Or of her stomping through strategically placed mud on her way to Clark Gable's waiting embrace in 1953's *Mogambo*.

But I have my own personal off-screen image of Ava. It occurred in 1963 while I was preparing *The Pink Panther* with Blake Edwards. It's of Ava disembarking an airplane in Paris, swaying her hips with flamenco sharpness. And with every sway of her hips, she emitted a string of increasingly colorful profanities.

And this, in a serpentine way, led to the casting of Peter Sellers as Inspector Jacques Clouseau.

And what did Ava's purple vocabulary have to do with *The Pink Panther*? During most movie productions, byzantine adventures occur in which things happen for the strangest reasons. Blake and I felt optimistic that we could make a shining *Pink Panther*. We did, but not without a few setbacks.

Casting the suave jewel thief was easy. David Niven, as charming off-screen as he was on, had the unforced elegance and casual charm perfect for the part. He had the ability to deliver a sarcastic line with bite and then cushion it with warmth.

Marty made a rare screen appearance as a gendarme in the opening scenes of *The Pink Panther*. Here he takes direction from Blake Edwards.

David Niven (left), the "Jewel Thief," and Marty, who is probably grinning at one of David's wry and witty anecdotes.

But what about Inspector Clouseau? Immediately we thought of Peter Sellers. But he was mired in preparation for Stanley Kubrick's *Dr. Strangelove*, and we did not want to be the target of the infamous Kubrick wrath. Even at that early point in his career, Kubrick was known as a master manipulator, who enjoyed putting producers and financiers in difficult situations. When *Eyes Wide Shut* was released four months after his 1999 death, I felt that somehow he was watching each aspect of the film's advance publicity, manipulating the potential moviegoer as smoothly as he manipulated actors and executives.

Another Clouseau possibility was Danny Kaye, no longer sure-fire box-office but still a phenomenal talent. Always at Danny's side was his ever-zealous, probably over-zealous wife Sylvia, whose influence on her husband could never be discounted.

As I expected, it was Sylvia, rather than Danny, who called me on the phone. What I didn't expect were her words.

"Tell me, Marty, where is the comedy? I have read the script and I can't find the comedy."

Sylvia probably sensed that I was seething on the other end of the line.

"Let's not bother talking about it, Sylvia," I said, with as much civility as I could muster. "Just send the script back. It would not be wise for this discussion to continue."

"Well, I just don't understand," she persisted. "Which is the comedy role, the inspector or the thief?"

She wound up sending the script back. Quickly.

Blake and I then settled on Peter Ustinov as Clouseau. Peter won an Oscar in 1960 for *Spartacus*

Peter Ustinov, the original choice for Inspector Clouseau. When Ava Gardner left, so did he.

Martin.
Just the way you
want me ....!!
C. C.

Claudia Cardinale, lovely and alluring, was a great asset on the set of *The Pink Panther*.

and would win another for *Topkapi* in 1964. His twinkly voice was altogether right for Clouseau. And he always seemed comfortable on the screen, which might make the Inspector's clumsiness all the more a comic contrast.

And so we were ready to start. We had David Niven and Peter Ustinov, and we had just signed Robert Wagner and Claudia Cardinale. We had been issued a starting date for our locations in Rome and Northern Italy, and the future of *The Pink Panther* looked unclouded.

There was, however, an important female role to be filled, that of Inspector Clouseau's chic but cheating wife. She had to be exotic, fashionable, and so desirable that Clouseau would gladly believe any lie she told him.

And at that time, we felt Madame Clouseau had to be Ava Gardner. Ava's days as a box-office diva had been in the previous decade, but she was still a household name who could be as exotic, fashionable and desirable as the part required. All audiences had to do was take one look at Ava's gorgeous pair of lips and they'd understand why Clouseau believed every lie they spoke.

Ava, dear Ava, had fled Hollywood to live in Spain, which she loved. She was reluctant to leave Madrid and wanted us to shoot the film there instead of Rome. I flew to Madrid to apply some friendly persuasion.

I wound up being so friendly that I bought dinner for her and fourteen of her closest friends. We went from restaurant to restaurant before she found one that satisfied her. And at each stop, she gathered more dinner companions.

She continued to be obstinate about moving the location to Madrid. The press had not always been kind to her, and she loathed the Italian paparazzi, who she felt could be avoided by filming in Madrid.

During the meal, she walked past me, grabbed a linen tablecloth and performed a wild flamenco step, shouting "Ole, Madrid!" Had anyone told me two hours earlier that I would attempt a flamenco step, I would have thought they were crazy. But I retrieved the tablecloth, managed a flamenco turn and responded, "Ole, Rome!"

Our eyes locked. There was no way we could change locations.

"We're all set in Rome," I said.

"Then unseat yourself," was her reply.

After much discussion, she agreed to play Madame Clouseau. But with a staggering list of perks.

At first we agreed to all her demands. Ava, a nocturnal creature to the core, wanted a twenty-four-hour limousine service, with two drivers. Gladly, Ava, gladly. She wanted a private cook from a mountain town in Italy. Well, fine, Ava. And she insisted on a fully staffed villa in Rome. Oh, all right, Ava. She demanded that we pay her favorite hairdresser to take a leave of absence from his shop in Manhattan and do her hair. OK, Ava, OK. When I wanted Yves St. Laurent to do her wardrobe, she for once readily agreed.

He agreed to postpone his spring collection but made his own request, one that turned Ava from purring pussycat to snarling tigress. He asked that since Ava would be on her way to Rome to start shooting, she stop off in Paris to be fitted. We told Ava of his request, expecting a volatile response.

What we got was vintage Gardner: "The son-of-a-bitch has a tape measure, doesn't he? Let him come to me!"

But finally Ava swallowed her pride. The idea of having an Yves St. Laurent wardrobe was appealing to her, and she agreed to stop off in Paris for the fitting. She implored us to make sure there would be no photographers. Or perhaps "implored" is too genteel a word. She muttered something like "woe be unto you if anyone knows I'm there," her silken voice more menacing than Vincent Price's.

There was no way to make such a guarantee. Before the plane landed, practically every photographer in Paris was stationed at the terminal. Word had leaked out that Ava Gardner was on the plane.

And then came the moment of unforgettable spectacle. There was Ava, with flashing eyes shining from her beautifully sculpted face, descending the plane with swiveling hips and vulgar expletives, each word-combination more inventive than the preceding one.

She cursed the photographers, only to be jeered at in return. She cursed me prolifically. Somehow I felt I could survive being cussed out by Ava Gardner. But she also cursed the driver and the luggage carriers, who were simply doing their jobs and had nothing to do with what she perceived as a betrayal.

We both remained silent as I took her to the Plaza Athenae. Her suite was filled with champagne and flowers, according to her request.

I spoke tersely. "There are your flowers. There is your champagne. Good night and goodbye."

For the next several hours, I thought hard about the Ava situation. Blake and I conferred about it at length and called the Mirisch Brothers in California. Their company was releasing *The Pink Panther* through United Artists. We came to a decision.

At two A.M., I slipped a note under her door saying it looked as though she didn't want to do the picture and she was being released from her obligation. The next day, I visited museums while she made $1,500 worth of phone calls to William Morris. Then she was gone.

Still, we were less than two weeks from shooting, and we had no wife for Inspector Clouseau. Thankfully, we found a warm, enigmatic beauty named Capucine, who had Ava's exotic qualities but made fewer demands.

And then, suddenly, we were without an Inspector Clouseau.

As a filmmaker, I learned never to underestimate the influence of a star's spouse. Mrs. Peter Ustinov was outraged that Ava had been fired and replaced with Capucine. She considered Ava a bona fide star and Capucine a nobody. With a nobody playing Ustinov's wife, she felt the film was reduced to a routine comedy of no artistic merit.

Peter listened to his wife, who was not one to quiet down. He left the picture. So now we had a wife for Inspector Clouseau, but no Clouseau. Shooting was to begin in less than a fortnight.

And then something happened that usually only happens on the screen, not behind the scenes. I spent the night following the Ustinov exodus tossing and turning, wondering who our Inspector Jacques Clouseau would be. A voice came to me in the middle of the night, distinctly advising me, "Give Peter Sellers another try."

I didn't have to ask the voice to repeat itself. In the back of my mind, I had never given up on Peter Sellers. His chameleon performances in films like 1959's *The Mouse That Roared*, in which he played three different characters, demonstrated his finesse for physical and verbal comedy. If less cuddly than Peter Ustinov, he was more flexible comedically. But Blake and I had despaired of obtaining Sellers' services, knowing he was busy preparing Kubrick's classic dark comedy *Dr. Strangelove*.

And this is where Sophia Loren enters the scene. Or, rather, the Loren allure enters to play an important part in *The Pink Panther*'s casting.

Sophia's career is an amazing one. Always adored by the public, she's a superstar without a long list of hit movies. But she didn't need anything as commonplace as a hit movie. As a woman and a love goddess, Sophia Loren was a smash hit.

And she remains fascinating. When I saw her on the 1999 Oscarcast, bestowing the screenwriting award on a frantic Roberto Benigni for *Life Is Beautiful*, she was spectacular. Her impact at the Oscars was so great, her face decorated the covers of national magazines shortly thereafter.

All of Sophia's costars fell in love with her. Cary Grant was obsessed with her for years. And in 1960, Peter Sellers made a film with Sophia Loren.

Marty with trench-coated Peter Sellers. Peter may look relaxed, but he was always looking over his shoulder.

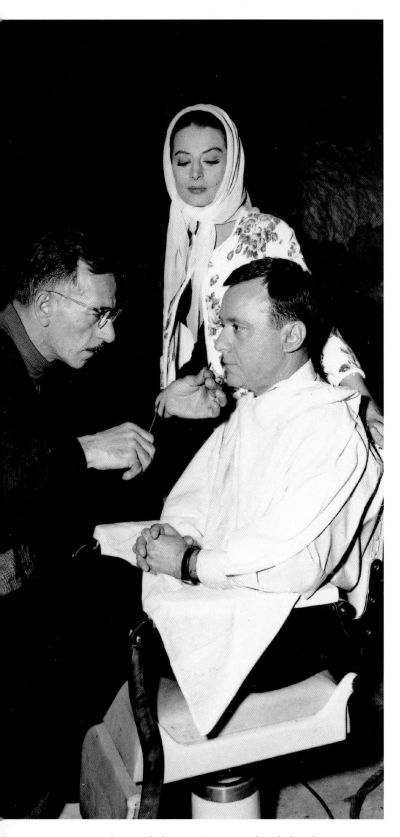

Capucine looks on as Marty gets made up for his role in *The Pink Panther*.

While watching Sophia and Peter frolic through the movie version of George Bernard Shaw's *The Millionairess*, I could tell that he was completely enthralled with her. Even three years after *The Millionairess* was released, word on the street was that Peter was so smitten with Sophia, he could hardly concentrate on his work. He was in an emotionally vulnerable frame of mind. Not only was he in the throes of Sophia-mania, but he was also bewildered when his own wife ran off with their interior decorator.

I arranged a London lunch with Peter and his agent Freddie Fields. When Peter slowly entered the Mirabel, he hardly looked like a sprightly comic actor. He was haggard and drawn. We sat down to what initially seemed a disastrous meeting. Peter's eyes were glazed over, his shoulders hunched. He was totally preoccupied, never looking anyone in the eye. Oblivious to all else, he kept scanning the room, as if searching forlornly for Sophia.

With deceptive casualness, I said, "I just got back from Rome."

Peter perked up instantly, and I realized this was the time for action. Asking Freddie to excuse us, I bid Peter follow me to the men's lounge. Once there, I grabbed him by the lapels of his jacket and said:

"Listen carefully, Peter, for I will say this once and never say it again. She's waiting for you."

The glaze left his eyes, and they gleamed with excitement and anticipation. His shoulders snapped to attention, and he assumed a pose as debonair as James Bond at a roulette wheel. He never feigned innocence. He never questioned the identity of the unnamed "she." He knew I knew.

It was a blatant manipulation on my part. I had never contacted Sophia on Peter's behalf and had no intention of doing so. But it was a perky Peter who strutted back to the table, delighted to become Inspector Clouseau. Of course the lure of Loren wasn't enough; he wanted a good business deal to go with it. We agreed to film all his scenes in six consecutive weeks, with the assurance of steep cash of 24,000 pounds a day for each day of overtime. After all, he would be returning to *Dr. Strangelove*, and Stanley Kubrick did not like to be kept waiting.

I don't know if Sophia realizes the role she played in Peter's casting. When her 1979 autobiography was published, Peter was upset that she devoted so little space to him.

When informed that Sellers felt slighted, the sagacious Sophia responded, "Knowing Peter as I do, he probably thinks I should call it *Peter and Me*."

Did Peter hold Sophia's absence against me? Not at all. Fortunately, Fran Jeffries looked somewhat like Sophia and knew how to placate a moody artist like Peter Sellers. Despite his Loren obsession, Peter willingly allowed himself to be placated.

Meanwhile, filming went harmoniously. Blake was a true slapstick scholar, having grown up with the films of Harold Lloyd, Charlie Chaplin, Harry Langdon, Al St. John, Buster Keaton, Laurel and Hardy. On the first day of shooting, Peter, who was always popping pills, leaned on a globe and accidentally knocked it down.

"Keep it in," Blake said with delight. After that, they conceived many slapstick routines that audiences loved.

The cast was great. Capucine was lovely and cooperative, though there was always a dark cloud of melancholia surrounding her. In 1990, when Erin-Jo and I learned of her suicide, we were saddened but somehow not surprised.

Robert Wagner was a delight, a genuinely sweet individual. After the end of his first marriage to Natalie Wood a year earlier, his career had lost some of its bounce, and he was grateful for the part. *The Pink Panther* became the inspiration for his hit TV series, *It Takes a Thief*.

Would the filming have been this happy with Ava as Madame Clouseau? I doubt it. Ava would have lent an acidic touch to the set, and her heart would have remained in Spain.

David Niven was the production's bulwark. A highly respected gentleman, he had achieved stardom in degrees. His contract called for top billing. But it became obvious that Peter was running away with the movie, giving a performance that exceeded even our most optimistic expectations. I broached David with the idea that he and Peter might alternate top billing, with David billed first in some countries and Peter billed first in the others.

"Not on your life, chum," he said, in his blithe David Niven diction. "I get first billing in all countries in every part of the world."

I couldn't blame him. He had worked hard to reach stardom, and naturally he wanted to protect his status. But Blake and I suddenly found ourselves with a problem. David was best known as a comedy star, which made his Oscar-winning performance in *Separate Tables* such a heart-wrenching contrast. Many of those comedies were charming but lightweight. We didn't want the public's first impression of *The Pink Panther* to be that it was the latest in the string of fluffy David Niven comedies.

And then Blake seized upon the idea of an animated Pink Panther. The unflappable feline would be featured in the print advertising campaign and would be displayed with the film's opening credits, becoming the first thing the public noticed as he merrily bounced and skipped to Henry Mancini's memorable theme song.

The film opened to great success, and with its release, a new star was born—the animated pink panther. But two other stars were responsible for Peter Sellers becoming Jacques Clouseau. I wound up wanting to thank Ava. As for Sophia, all I can say is, Viva, Loren!

14

Comics Can Make You Cry

~

In the glorious human landscape of show business, comedians are the most difficult personalities with whom to sit and have a normal conversation. People like Mickey Rooney and Jerry Lewis never stop performing. They could turn the eating of a breakfast roll into a comic routine. And sometimes you just want to go ahead and eat your breakfast roll.

There are, of course, happy exceptions. Jack Lemmon is a generous, warm performer. David Niven was as elegant and witty away from the camera as he was when being filmed. Jimmy Durante was a wonderful human being although he never would tell me who "Mrs. Calabash" was. She remains the mystery woman to whom Jimmy tipped his hat, closing each performance, "And good night, Mrs. Calabash, wherever you are."

Andy Griffith holds a special place in my affections. This country boy from the South went from hit recording ("What It Was, Was Football") to hit Broadway show (*No Time for Sergeants*) to

the hit movie version of *No Time for Sergeants* to the hit *Andy Griffith Show* television series. But his greatest triumph was as a human being.

I took delight in being among those who thought he would be perfect in *No Time for Sergeants*, the Army comedy in which his hilarious, tender performance of vulnerable, well-meaning Will Stockdale made him a Broadway star in 1955. It was produced by noted Shakespearean actor Maurice Evans and directed by Morton Da Costa, a friend and client. Even with those credentials, it was almost ready to fold during Philadelphia tryouts.

Da Costa called, told me the audience's response to the play, and asked if I had any suggestions.

"The play is a solid play, but it needs to be something more," I said. "It needs to be a funny show, a hilarious show. Let's bring in a play doctor who can shower the show with one-liners."

Da Costa knew that Joseph Stein could write lines that fed right into Andy's comic skills. And

Dean Martin and Jerry Lewis, taking the world by storm. (*Dallas Morning News* archives)

while Joe worked on one-liners, Da Costa concentrated on developing the characters. The result was a Broadway smash. Maurice Evans always felt indebted to Joe Stein, as we all did. Joe had a nimble wit that would have made him a natural for classic television sitcoms. Although he was happy doctoring the shows of others, his greatest success would come under his own name in 1964. It was the remarkable *Fiddler on the Roof.*

After the hit stage and screen versions of *No Time for Sergeants,* Andy would make several more movies, including *Onionhead,* a fast spin-off of *No Time for Sergeants,* released only months later in 1958. The following year, he returned to Broadway in the modestly successful *Destry Rides Again.* None of his non-*Sergeants* movies was a box-office hit, but at least *A Face in the Crowd,* Elia Kazan's 1957 exposé of media manipulation, ranks as a classic. Among other things, it showed that Andy, always likable in real life, didn't insist on playing likable characters on-screen.

I appreciated Andy's perspective and his sharp self-evaluation. Unlike many stars, including comedy diva Lucille Ball, he never considered movies the height of a show business career. He was aware of his own limitations.

I remember sitting with him in a hotel lobby in 1960 when he suddenly said, "I think there is a better place for me in this new TV series than in movies."

"Don't you think you can become a major movie star?" I said, caught off-guard by his honesty.

"He's gone," Andy said simply. "His time in the movies has passed on."

"What do you mean?"

"Marty, Will Rogers is gone. Anything I could do in movies would be a poor substitute for what Will Rogers did."

"You could be his Shirley Temple," I replied. Andy, as always, had the good grace to laugh.

Andy's prophecy about his television show proved wonderfully correct. *The Andy Griffith Show,* which premiered in 1960, was a home-run series, the harbinger of such rustic comedy fare as *Petticoat Junction, The Beverly Hillbillies,* and *Green Acres.* And it placed him in a position of power that he never abused. He used his rank as a means to give to others rather than luxuriating in being given to.

So many artists are so taken with themselves that they fail to appreciate the work done by others, who often sacrificed hours of their own time. But not Andy. He kept the same steadfast manager, Richard Link, who worked diligently on his behalf.

He remembered Don Knotts from a small role in *No Time for Sergeants* and made him an important part of the series. He took an active interest in each cast and crew member. He helped Frances Bavier's Aunt Bee become a part of Americana, and he spotlighted Jim Nabors's Gomer Pyle so generously that the character became strong enough for its own show in 1964. And he lovingly nurtured the talents of young Ron Howard, now a director of great importance.

Later in his career, Andy would suffer illnesses that kept him confined to his North Carolina home. But in 1986, when he was ready to work again, the television show *Matlock* was fashioned for him. As always, he won raves, this time as a wily lawyer in seersucker suits.

Phil Silvers is another personal favorite. I discovered Phil in burlesque and helped promote him

Andy Griffith, a star who lent a helping hand to Elvis Presley, Jim Nabors, and Ron Howard, was an enthusiastic judge of other people's talent and a realistic judge of his own.

To
warmly
appreciated
Andy
Griffith

for the Broadway show *Top Banana*. His character was based on Milton Berle, and Phil played him with rambunctious humor, bravado, and a touch of humanity that won audiences over.

I felt a sense of pride when *The Phil Silvers Show* became the toast of television. The wonderful qualities of his stage performances were enhanced on TV screens, and *The Phil Silvers Show* was a howling success in 1955. His character of Master Sergeant Ernie Bilko was a comic triumph. Years later, when an unnecessary movie adaptation was made, even such a talented comic actor as Steve Martin couldn't erase the memory of Phil's Bilko. There could never be another Phil Silvers.

Other comic figures are filled with complexities. I enjoyed working with Jackie Gleason on *Soldier in the Rain*, but I always understood that he considered himself The Maestro and was as temperamental and self-centered as any musical diva.

Peter Sellers should have been on top of the world after *The Pink Panther* was a worldwide smash. But Peter would never allow himself to be comfortable at such lofty heights. He would always be looking out of the corner of his eye for a disastrous banana peel.

Acutely aware of being Jewish, Peter saw anti-Semitism everywhere and felt its sting, whether the prejudice was real or imagined. He was suspicious of what would happen next, and he was always on pills. Sadly, for a man who gave pleasure to audiences across the world, he could never enjoy his own moment of pleasure. He once remarked that he believed in the adage, "Don't bask too much in the flow of victory. Trouble is just around the corner."

Milton Berle, on the other hand, was afraid of nothing and nobody. Except his mother. A tall, arrogant, and formidable woman, Sandra Berle was known universally as Mother Berle. She earned her son's eternal gratitude and internal fear. She

believed that she was the only one in the world who understood Milton. She always sided with him, and she was convinced that the rest of the world was against him. Everyone at the television studio and at the William Morris Agency, where I was an executive during television's early days, rejoiced when she stayed home. But it was a rare occasion when she did.

Uncle Miltie, as Milton was known, was undisputed King of Television during the early 1950s. With the enormous popularity of Tuesday night's *The Milton Berle Show*, he was responsible for selling more television sets than any other performer. Despite being welcomed into the living rooms of millions of Americans via the small screen, Milton longed for big-screen success. He wanted to be a movie star. He made several films, including 1949's hotly hyped *Always Leave Them Laughing*. None of them was a hit. Their failure haunted Milton, and his mother haunted us.

She screamed, "If Bob Hope can be a big movie star, with that nose of his, why can't you make a big movie star out of Milton???" Her wailings echoed through the corridors of the William Morris Agency. And everyone breathed a sigh of relief when Mother Berle had finally left the building.

Did Milton resent his mother's meddling? Probably not. After Sandra's death, he married Ruth, a strong and confrontational woman who resembled Mother Berle in her ferocious championship of the man she loved.

Milton always had popular guests on his show. Always desiring to be center stage, he frequently cut in on their routines. The most recent footage I saw of Milton was saddening. He was attending Frank Sinatra's funeral and frequently looked over his shoulder imploringly, as if hoping someone would recognize him. He's still a legend, but it must have been painful to go from spending Tuesday nights in America's living rooms to being just another face at a crowded funeral.

Danny Kaye, a great talent, was one of the most difficult people to be in the same room with. Sylvia Fine, his devoted wife, was also a troubled human being. She suffered greatly being Mrs. Danny Kaye. Danny dallied. He dallied frequently and with some diversity. But Sylvia understood his psychological roots. She understood his torment and his constant need to prove himself in every possible way.

Most comedians need to be petted, to be stroked, to be reassured. Danny was another story. When he walked into a room, his attitude was "We both know how brilliant I am! Aren't you lucky to be in the same room with me!" He was willing to include the other person in acknowledging his own brilliance.

In the early 1950s, Sid Caesar's hit series, *Your Show of Shows*, in which Sid and Imogene Coca gained comic immortality, was the gathering place of future comedy geniuses.

Aside from Sid, Imogene, and Carl Reiner, the behind-the-scenes characters included an outgoing, pleasant young man named Neil Simon, a shy and nervous fellow named Woody Allen, and a bombastic talent named Mel Brooks.

They worked together happily and gave the impression that they loved each other, which they probably did. They were at the beginning of their careers, with their talents being showcased in the omnipotent new medium of television. There was friendly competition, but no jealousy. In those days of live television, so much was involved with simply putting on a weekly show, there was no time for jealousy.

Mel had a great need to be needed. When *Your Show of Shows* came to a close in 1954, he had a difficult time finding a showcase for his remarkable, high-voltage humor. And without a showcase, Mel is not a happy man. Finally, his comic

recording of "The Two-Thousand-Year-Old Man" became a sensation. And he conquered the movie world with the comic punch of *Blazing Saddles* and *Young Frankenstein.*

But within a few years, his luck once again seemed to desert him. For the last fifteen years, his films, such as 1993's *Robin Hood: Men in Tights*, have been disappointing. He has borne these critical and commercial mishaps with dignity. But a man as eager to please as Mel could never be content occupying middle ground. He has to be at the top of the mountain, and he ascended once again in 2001 with his smash hit stage adaptation of his first movie, 1968's *The Producers.*

Jerry Lewis, whose career has known both peaks and valleys, scored a hit playing the devil in the 1996 revival of *Damn Yankees.* I was glad for his success because I know that failure does not sit well with Jerry. Yet, the absolute truth is that nothing sits well with Jerry.

Jerry as the devil? That fits. As I have watched him through the years, the very nature of Jerry's character is one of devilment. He finds it hard to share, to think of anyone but himself, and he was far from popular on a personal basis. Despite his public displays of charity, such as the *Jerry Lewis Marathon* every Labor Day weekend, he always seemed a mean figure, and I could never see him as a lovable individual. But I can see him playing Mr. Applegate in *Damn Yankees.* Maybe it's type-casting.

Most comedians have no time for family. Their profession, and by extension the audience, are their family. During my MCA days in the early 1940s, I represented the legendary Ed Wynn. In his prime, there was no one bigger than Ed. He was king of vaudeville. He was one of the first kings of radio. All his fans felt they knew him personally. His family felt they never knew him at all.

His son Keenan Wynn costarred in my production of *The Great Race.* But I was to meet

Keenan earlier under more dramatic circumstances. I was in New York in the early 1940s when I got a frantic call from Ed. He pleaded with me to go to Boston, where Keenan was appearing in a play.

"I'm afraid Keenan is doing something rash," Ed said. "He's been so depressed lately."

"Something rash" turned out to be a grim understatement. When I got to Keenan's hotel, he was on the window ledge, ready to jump. I coaxed him back inside, telling him that he had a great deal to offer the world, that he was more than just Ed Wynn's son.

But depression was to follow him all his life. He and his vivacious wife Evie took Van Johnson under their wing, and Evie later left Keenan for Van. Keenan and Van themselves were locked in an intense love/hate relationship.

Ed always felt responsible for Keenan's fits of depression. But some of Ed's remarks stung. Keenan had a successful career as a comic sidekick to Metro-Goldwyn-Mayer stars, frequently to Van Johnson himself. Ed had another, more dismissive way of describing his son's professional chores: "When Esther Williams dives into a pool, Keenan's the one who gets splashed," Ed said.

Ed genuinely cared about Keenan, but he could never handle a serious situation. His life was dedicated to his career. He avoided his family, unable to handle any of the entanglements that come with family life. He knew Keenan was depressed but wouldn't allow himself to come to grips with how deep the despondency went.

Among my memories of comic actors, one of my happiest is joining Lucille Ball and Desi Arnaz on their honeymoon. That was the only time I saw them completely happy.

They had just starred in the movie version of Rodgers and Hart's *Too Many Girls*, directed by George Abbott. Despite the Abbott name, the musical wasn't an A-movie. It was more like a B-plus movie. George Abbott may have been a Broadway legend, but Hollywood has its own hierarchy.

It was shortly after Thanksgiving of 1940, and Lucy and Desi were in a holiday dreamland. They were in what they hoped would be an important picture, and they had fallen in love while making the movie. In truth, neither was ready to marry. To a major extent, Lucy was married to Lucy, and Desi was married to Desi. But in true show business fashion, they married while touring with a famous newspaper columnist, Louella Parsons, who was the powerful, fire-breathing, and extremely vindictive columnist for William Randolph Hearst's newspaper empire.

Louella also had a popular radio show, and she toured movie theaters in major metropolitan areas, accompanied by aspiring stars eager for the exposure. She had chosen Lucy and Desi for this trip, with Lucy singing while Desi played the bongo drums. Louella and her entourage, including Lucy and Desi, settled briefly in Detroit, which was in the midst of a beautiful holiday snowfall.

I was in New York when Desi called me to have dinner to celebrate their marriage. When my plane landed in Detroit, the radiantly happy couple was there to greet me in a limousine.

We started to drive. Where we were headed, I did not know.

One hour passed.

"How far are we going?" I finally asked. I thought I had just come for dinner and nothing more. "Not far at all," they giggled in unison.

More than another hour passed, and we found ourselves at the stunning winter chalet of a Detroit automobile magnate. It was then that the romantic fact dawned on me: I was nonplussed to discover that I was sharing Lucille Ball and Desi Arnaz's honeymoon weekend.

You couldn't ask for a more picturesque setting. But I had no clothes, except for overnight wear. That didn't matter. All we needed was sweatsuits. A cook appeared as if on cue, and each meal was exquisitely prepared. For two and one-half days, we hibernated in a winter wonderland.

And for those two and one-half days, I never heard a cross word between Lucy and Desi. They were very open about their amour. I would hear their sweet murmurings as I slept on a wonderful bed on the chalet's enclosed balcony.

We joshed with each other and frolicked in the snow. We took sleigh rides. We drove through the chalet grounds in a surrey with a fringe on top. Three years later, *Oklahoma!* would open its record-breaking Broadway run, making the phrase "The Surrey With the Fringe on Top" a part of Americana. Whenever I would hear the song, I would think of Lucy and Desi and their all-too-brief bliss.

In their own way, they were as haunted a couple as Vivien Leigh and Laurence Olivier. Desi was the love of Lucy's life and the hell of her life. She would be in despair when she knew she had lost him for good.

Both Lucy and Desi were plagued. Lucy had a frantic need to be appreciated, to be on the A-list professionally. Desi became an alcoholic.

Before becoming a television queen, Lucy was a second banana under contract to RKO Radio Studio. She was considered more of a B-movie actress than an A-movie star, a fact that horrified her. She craved importance. Even after costarring with Henry Fonda in 1942's *The Big Street*, she was not embraced by the A-list, and she became even more obsessed with obtaining stardom. Without a doubt she deserved stardom. She was the most gifted physical clown in the business.

Then, during the golden years of *I Love Lucy*

in the early 1950s, she finally received the importance and acceptance she desperately sought. As a television star, she never hesitated to make demands. She was very important—and very, very busy. She had her own studio, Desilu. And being a busy, important star brought her some measure of peace. But even at the height of her truly historical TV years, she still felt the sting of never having been an A-list movie star.

In truth, she was not a person you would want to spend a great deal of time with—unless you were interested in hearing all about Lucy. Lucy was absorbed with the career and the growing myth of Lucille Ball. She was absorbed with Desi Arnaz primarily as Lucille Ball's husband and lover. Yet she was heartbroken at his constant philandering.

Total peace was not in their makeup even during their television heyday. At that time, they were also under a movie contract to MGM, and Desi longed to be a movie matinee idol with a fervor that almost surpassed Lucy's bygone dreams of movie stardom. He was devastated when MGM gave its prime Latin Lover roles to tall, macho Fernando Lamas. It's difficult to imagine Desi waltzing with Lana Turner in *The Merry Widow*, as Mr. Lamas did, but that's exactly what he wanted to do. Desi did not have a champion among the MGM executives, and personal success often hinged on who was rooting for you in the executive quarters.

Lucy was smarter than Desi in every way. But with her persistent supervision, she allowed him to give the appearance of handling their business as well as Desilu Productions. That was their way of showing MGM that Desi really was a big man after all.

As with many comic actors, their personal lives could make you cry.

15

Lemmon, Curtis, and the Great Race

~

I love comedy and have great professional respect for comic actors, starting with the vaudevillians I watched as a child. No film shows my love of comedy more than *The Great Race*.

Did all the critics love it? Some did, some didn't. But audiences across the globe cheered it.

Whenever I see the movie, a huge smile decorates my face. The smile is based on what I'm watching and what I'm remembering. The smile has a twinge of the bittersweet. *The Great Race* marked the end of my collaboration with Blake Edwards. Happily, it was not the end of our friendship, which remains warm. But it signaled a conclusion to our cinematic collaborations. Fittingly, it was a hilarious and spectacular finale.

The Great Race's cast was spectacular, too: Jack Lemmon, Tony Curtis, Natalie Wood, Peter Falk, Keenan Wynn, Dorothy Provine, Arthur O'Connell, and Vivian Vance, the beloved "Ethel" of *I Love Lucy*.

My friendship with Jack Lemmon started in 1950, when I was at the William Morris Agency, and he was a client. I always felt Jack's last name was perversely amusing. A sour lemon he is not. He remains one of the sweetest souls in the business.

Movies beckoned him early, but the agency's Charles Baker, a smart and intuitive individual, didn't encourage him to go west. Charlie was afraid that if Jack went to Hollywood so soon in his career, he would be just another dime-a-dozen juvenile lead. Charlie wanted him to gain experience in summer stock, theater, and live television, which was proving an invaluable training ground for young actors. Finally in 1954, when Charlie and I agreed that young Mr. Lemmon was ready to head west, I negotiated with Columbia's fearsome Harry Cohn a deal that is now known as the Lemmon Contract.

The small print allowed Jack to leave Hollywood twice during his contract period for

In the shadow of the Eiffel Tower, *The Great Race*'s villain Jack Lemmon sneers over the shoulders of pure-as-snow Tony Curtis and the coiffed and lovely Natalie Wood.

At the start of *The Great Race* everyone was smiling: (left to right) Jack Warner, Tony Curtis, Blake Edwards, Henry Mancini, Jack Lemmon, Marty. (Courtesy of the Academy of Motion Picture Arts and Sciences)

Broadway excursions. Cohn, with his short-sighted ego and sense of omnipotence, felt that once Jack tasted the pleasures of Hollywood, he would forsake the East Coast. I took some delight in encouraging Cohn to think so, knowing all the while that Jack was anxious to learn as much as he could from the legitimate theater.

So Jack returned to the stage, and growl though Cohn might, there was nothing he could do about it. Jack was determined to learn from soundstages, too, and by the time he made *Mister Roberts* in 1955, he was a remarkably versatile young actor.

He stayed on *Mister Roberts*'s set at all times. Even when he wasn't on call, he observed from the sidelines, learning everything he could from the

star-packed cast of Henry Fonda, James Cagney, and William Powell, and from the film's two directors, John Ford, who became ill after beginning production, and Mervyn LeRoy, who completed the project. Hank Fonda and Bill Powell were particularly helpful to the eager young actor.

Having been trained in the theater, Jack was accustomed to giving a heightened performance that would project across the footlights to the back row of the playhouse. Hank and Bill playfully urged him to lighten up on his projection. They must have made their point. Jack's performance as Ensign Pulver earned his first Oscar. His second would come eighteen years later with the intense *Save the Tiger*.

Along the way, he made many classics, including Billy Wilder's *Some Like It Hot*, which Erin-Jo and I consider the greatest comedy ever made. AFI voters agreed; when the American Film Institute released its list of the Hundred Greatest American Comedies in 2000, *Some Like It Hot* was No. 1. Released in 1959, it still carries a wonderful element of surprise.

Jack never forgot his stage roots. In 1960, the same year he triumphed in Wilder's *The Apartment*, he returned to Broadway with *Face of a Hero*, playing the role he created on television's *Playhouse 90*. Few other actors would have left Hollywood at such a peak in their careers to return to the stage.

Charlie Baker had done a superb job of shaping and molding Jack, and he also aided the

The Great Race boasted the custard pie fight to end all custard pie fights. Only Tony Curtis's clean-cut hero, The Great Leslie (center), escaped without a smear.

For Marty —
The Compact Producers
Love,
Jack

careers of Angela Lansbury and Walter Matthau, with whom Jack formed a memorable acting partnership and enduring friendship. Enduring friendships come easily to someone of Jack's personality. When I learned of Charlie Baker's death, I instantly called Jack. He was bereft, saying he had been thinking of Charlie just before he heard of his death. Jack is the kind who never forgets.

Lemmon and Matthau were a comedy team that lasted decades, and when Walter died in 2000, Jack felt like he had lost a brother. Jack and Tony Curtis also made an ideal duo. In *Some Like It Hot*, their wiggles made screen history. They reteamed in 1965 in *The Great Race*, with each showing utmost respect for the other's talent. They understood each other's strengths, grasped each other's acting rhythms, and never tried to upstage the other.

Off-screen, they were opposites. Jack is a natural giver; Tony, a consummate taker. In *Some Like It Hot*, Tony had been billed before Jack, and they shared the comic load. In *The Great Race*, Jack was billed before Tony and carried the comedy, while Tony shouldered the romantic portions with Natalie Wood. Tony, who always found something to be chagrined about, was indignant throughout most of the shooting.

In telling the story of a round-the-world race between Tony's toothsome hero and Jack's venomous villain, *The Great Race* was shot in Vienna, Paris, Salzburg, and Kentucky before ending up at Warner Bros. in Burbank. During the difficult locations, Jack made only one request. He wanted a certain hotel suite when his family joined him in Vienna. On the other hand, Tony made many requests—including the exact same hotel suite Jack had specified. Tony checked into the hotel early. I came to evict him before Jack arrived.

Peeking around Marty, the actress Felicia Farr (aka Mrs. Jack Lemmon). (Photograph by Bill Crespinel)

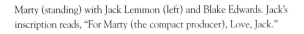

Marty (standing) with Jack Lemmon (left) and Blake Edwards. Jack's inscription reads, "For Marty (the compact producer), Love, Jack."

Marty takes a stroll with Christina Kaufman, Tony Curtis's wife at the time of *The Great Race*.
The Curtises' newborn baby came in handy when Tony wanted a particular hotel suite.

Tony was the father of a newborn child. And when I entered the suite, he was posing, babe in arms.

"Do you have the nerve to evict my infant and me?" he implored.

Poor Jack. He was not happy, but he resigned himself to Tony's act. He realized some things are not worth fighting over and, too, I think he comprehended Tony's resentment of his comic stature.

What a great race that movie was! Natalie had been a hard-working actress since childhood.

It's amazing how many classic films she contributed to: portraying a child in 1947's *Miracle on 34th Street*, and a teenager in both 1955's *Rebel Without a Cause* and 1956's *The Searchers*.

West Side Story and *Splendor in the Grass*, both released in 1961, turned her into Hollywood royalty, a position she sought staunchly to maintain. A determined woman, she never seemed happy or content, except perhaps for much of the time she shared with Robert Wagner.

On *The Great Race*, she was acutely aware

Tony Curtis (right) poses with Marty at the gates of the Schönbrunn Palace in Vienna.

Blake Edwards (left) and Marty confer on the set of *The Great Race*.

that her role was not as substantial as those of the two male stars. But she knew it would be a big picture, and she was happy to be with Jack and Tony. She was determined to be treated as their equal, and in her single-mindedness, she sometimes did not act like the star she imagined herself to be.

On one of the first days of shooting, Natalie was not needed on the set. Jack, Tony, and Peter Falk were in perfect position, as was the cavalcade of vintage cars needed for the scene. Over the loudspeaker came the ominous words: "Miss Wood would like to see Mr. Jurow in her dressing room."

When I entered her dressing room, she stood posing as dramatically as Tony in that Vienna hotel suite. Instead of a baby, she carried a telephone extension cord.

In great detail, she stated that she had just returned from Jack's and Tony's dressing rooms, where she had measured their telephone extension

Marty busses a gorgeously gowned Natalie Wood on the set of *The Great Race*, Paris, 1962. (Photograph by Bob Willoughby)

cords. Just as she suspected, their cords were longer than hers.

"Is that what you called me away from the set for?" I asked.

"Absolutely," came her answer. "In all things, I must be on the same level as Jack and Tony. I don't want to start this film giving away an ounce of my position."

"Well, Natalie, I will certainly take care of the cord calamity. And I will take care of something else, too."

Let me digress to say that during some of *The Great Race*'s filming, Tony had started a luncheon club, for which he prepared the menu and acted as maitre d'. Natalie, Jack, Blake, and I were always included, and invitations to the luncheon were coveted among cast and crew.

"I'm placing you in a state of coventry, Natalie," I said, surprising even myself at my schoolmaster tones as I referred to the form of discipline that ostracizes an errant youth from a peer group.

I spoke the fatal verdict: "You can no longer come to the luncheons."

She suddenly seemed as vulnerable as the little girl from *Miracle on 34th Street* who wanted to believe in Santa Claus.

"You would do that to me?" she said, her eyes suddenly as wistful as in the farewell scene from *Splendor in the Grass.*

My stern facade began to crack a little, and then we both threw our heads back and laughed.

She agreed, up to a point, that she had not behaved with complete maturity. But she remained obdurate in her desire for parity with her costars. Before we parted company on that fateful morning, I spoke the words that would soothe her wounded ego: "Natalie, I will make every effort to see that you are not harmed in any further manner."

The Great Race was a comedy of misadventures, both on-screen and off. There was the time Blake ordered breakfast in Salzburg. He stated nonchalantly that he would like bacon and eggs.

"We do not serve bacon and eggs," responded the waiter in a thick Austrian accent that made Blake wonder if he had heard correctly.

"Do you have bacon?" inquired a bewildered Blake.

"Yes."

"Do you have eggs?"

"Yes."

"Well, then, combine them," said Blake, his bewilderment turning to exasperation.

The waiter spoke slowly, but his manner indicated his patience was limited. "We do have bacon. We do have eggs. We do not serve them together."

It was a scene to rival Jack Nicholson's famous chicken-salad sequence in 1970's *Five Easy Pieces.* And the result was that a vituperative, explosive Blake went without breakfast that morning.

It was always my habit to awaken each day and mentally prepare myself for little footpads of danger that might occur. But nothing quite prepared me for our one day of shooting in a castle in Vienna. We came in one day early to get everything as ready as possible. Blake suddenly decided it was absolutely necessary to have forty dancing couples in the big ballroom in the castle.

This had never been indicated in our storyboards. I spent the night in search of forty dancing couples suitable for a grand Viennese ballroom. The muses smiled on me that night. Before filming the next morning, I actually located a club of dancers. And, yes, they were adept at the Viennese waltz.

A producer must be both a nurturing and a demanding parent, with the savvy to know when to be which. A producer must also be an inspira-

Professor Fate (Jack Lemmon) cozies up to Producer Marty, who is not amused.

Marty worrying over whether Blake could complete the filming of the spectacular ballroom scene at the Hofburg Palace in time—they had permission to use the palace only until 3 p.m.

tion and an accountant, sometimes simultaneously. By the time *The Great Race* landed at the Warner Bros. studio, the budget had grown from $8 million to $11 million, an enormous amount at the time. Blake frequently felt lengthy rehearsals were necessary, which added to the cost. When we started shooting at the studio, we realized we lacked the money to build several vintage cars that were essential to the scene.

Mr. Warner, still the studio head, huffed, "Make out with what you have. I'm not giving you any more money to build some cars."

What to do, what to do . . .

Ray Firestone was the head of the tire company that bore his family name. He had offices around the world, and I had read that he was going to San Francisco for a meeting. His brother Leonard lived in Los Angeles and was an acquain-

After 3 P.M., a jubilant Marty—"We made it!"

tance of mine. I called Leonard and prevailed upon him to ask Ray to stop in Los Angeles and give me five minutes, just five minutes of his time.

Prior to going to San Francisco, Ray stopped off at the studio, complete with entourage. He was a short man, and we stood eye-to-eye.

"Mr. Firestone," I said, staring into his unblinking eyes. "In publicizing our wonderful picture, in its marketing and advertising, would you like me to say, 'It's a good year for *The Great Race*'?"

I knew, of course, that Goodyear and Firestone were locked in an intense rivalry, and I waited for his response.

Without missing a beat, he said, "What do you need?"

I instantly replied, "I need $100,000 to finish building the necessary cars. I will place the name of Firestone on the tires. The name Firestone will appear at least nine times in the film."

Our five-minute meeting occurred on a Friday. On Tuesday, $100,000 was ours. And the name Firestone found its way into *The Great Race*. It was product placement born of necessity.

Despite the inevitable zany moments, there was enormous warmth on the set of *The Great Race*, and that feeling permeated the picture. Peter Falk was an exquisite master of the pool cue, and both Jack and Tony were pigeons in his hands. We traveled with a pool table, courtesy of the Brunswick family, and Jack and Tony lost hundreds of dollars to Peter.

By the end of the filming, Blake's agents and managers had convinced him that he should be his own producer, that he no longer needed me to oversee his productions. In my not entirely unprejudiced viewpoint, a hands-on producer is essential. Elia Kazan did some of his best work, including

At Warner Bros. studio in 1962, Marty (left) and art director Fernando Carrere discuss details of what kind of heroic, snow-white car would be suitable for *The Great Race*'s The Great Leslie.

A Streetcar Named Desire, for strong producers, such as *Streetcar*'s Charles Feldman. Joseph L. Mankiewicz made *All About Eve* and *A Letter to Three Wives* as Darryl F. Zanuck's personal productions. His subsequent work never matched those landmark films.

I like to think that I could have been beneficial to Blake's later films, but at the time, it was not too difficult to say goodbye. Still, we have remained stalwart friends. After all, we gave birth to *Breakfast at Tiffany's*, *The Pink Panther*, and *The Great Race*. It was, by and large, a happy creative marriage, and our cinematic progeny still shine.

Blake Edwards poses in front of "Professor Fate's" trick car—especially designed with a cannon and elevator seats for *The Great Race* at Warner Bros. studio.

Marty (left) and art director Fernando Carrere with The Great Leslie's car, a Firestone custom car complete with Firestone tires, for *The Great Race*.

Lunch break on the set of *The Great Race*—the exclusive game of pool. Tony Curtis (second from left) waits his turn as Jack Lemmon shoots. Blake Edwards is in the dark glasses, Peter Falk at far right.

Beneath the Eiffel Tower, cast and crew celebrate "finis" of *The Great Race*.

16

Spinning Wheels

~

I've been pleased with magical teamings in the movies I've produced. There were magic moments between Peter Sellers and David Niven in *The Pink Panther*, between Shirley MacLaine and Jack Nicholson in *Terms of Endearment*, between Jack Lemmon and Tony Curtis in *The Great Race*, between Audrey Hepburn and the entire city of Manhattan in *Breakfast at Tiffany's*.

And there was magic between Jackie Gleason and Steve McQueen in 1963's *Soldier in the Rain*. It was an extraordinary pairing, Maestro Gleason and maverick McQueen. And it should have been an extraordinary film. But various factors prevented it from reaching its full potential. A modest box-office success when released, it is now considered a cult film. But what a movie it might have been!

It was based on an early novel by William Goldman, who would become one of our greatest screenwriters with such credits as *Butch Cassidy and the Sundance Kid* in 1969 and *All the President's Men* in 1976. *Soldier in the Rain* had the same sharply observed characters as his later works. The offbeat

comedy-drama took place on an army base, where a master sergeant (Jackie) is hero-worshipped by an awe-struck inferior (Steve).

I liked the book and brought it to Blake Edwards's attention. He and I had a very amicable relationship following the successes of *Breakfast at Tiffany's* and *The Pink Panther*. We purchased *Soldier in the Rain* and quickly cast Jackie and Steve, two amazing if incongruous figures.

Steve had survived a hard and impoverished childhood. The experience had toughened him, but it also gave him the subtle vulnerability that was perfect for *Soldier in the Rain*. He scored a hit in the television series *Wanted: Dead or Alive* and was determined to reach a position of prominence in movies. Nothing could stand in his way. Yet he stopped short of ruthlessness. (I know the difference between determination and ruthlessness. After all, I knew Kirk Douglas.)

Steve believed in commitment, in keeping his word. He also believed that those around him should understand his impulses. He was not so

Steve McQueen (left) and Jackie Gleason could have made beautiful music in *Soldier in the Rain*, but disparate acting techniques and various production problems struck discordant notes.

much interested in moviemaking as he was in spinning wheels.

He was a master on wheels. Whenever you watched him ride an unusual motorcycle or motorbike, it was obvious that he craved a life of action and adventure. This would be reflected in such films as *The Magnificent Seven* (1960), *The Great Escape* (1963), *The Sand Pebbles* (1966), *Bullitt* (1968), and *The Getaway* (1972). He loved taking risks on his cycles, but he curbed his passion while filming. He knew I feared losing him every time he drove away in a cloud of dust.

He was a likable man, but he frequently seemed to be overcompensating. With both women and wheels, he might have found a grown-up substitute for the fun he had missed as a child. His love affair with Ali MacGraw, which started when they costarred in *The Getaway* and culminated in a brief, turbulent marriage, made news across the world. The fact that their affair started while Ali was still married to Robert Evans, the powerful producer who had shepherded her *Love Story* smash, added to Steve's macho image.

If Steve was Mr. Adventure, Jackie was Mr. Showman. He grew up in the world of show business. He tasted everything from burlesque to nightclubs to stage, radio, musicals, recordings, and of course television. I admired him in each outlet of his enormous talent.

He was also a composer and conductor, with a love of classical music. He had conquered all aspects of the entertainment world except motion pictures, and he was eager that *Soldier in the Rain* would fill that void.

As an impresario, he was best at selling himself. He would invite eight people to dinner and then leave without picking up the check. Perhaps he thought his company was enough. And, in many ways, it was. Yet there's no denying that he had a large, rotund ego and that he would not hesitate to vilify those who displeased him. Extremely self-centered, he could be a formidable opponent.

At first everything seemed to fall into place with *Soldier in the Rain*. I was certain that Blake, with his knack for comedy mixed with human warmth, could direct the film beautifully. Both Jackie and Steve were aware of Blake's and my track record and were eager to work with us. And then Blake dropped a bombshell.

Instead of *Soldier in the Rain*, he decided to direct another Inspector Clouseau comedy, *A Shot in the Dark*, to take advantage of *The Pink Panther's* huge success. I was heartbroken at Blake's decision. But in this business you must learn that personal feelings don't matter when it comes to career and opportunity. We all bend and sway in different ways.

I had been so certain that Blake would direct, I had done the unthinkable: To placate Jackie's obsessive need for control, I had given him the right to choose the director if Blake decided against the project. So now Jackie was in the primary position that he so unabashedly loved. He had enjoyed one of his strongest noncomedic roles in the movie version of *Requiem for a Heavyweight* and wanted its director, Ralph Nelson, to handle *Soldier in the Rain*.

Ralph was a fine director of drama, but he lacked the deft comic touch necessary for *Soldier in the Rain*. With Blake directing, the results would have been memorable. Blake willingly spent hours helping us with the film's editing. But, in truth, he was not sorry to leave the incendiary duo of McQueen and Gleason.

What a pair! It would be hard to find two actors with more disparate techniques. Like Frank Sinatra and Bing Crosby, Jackie liked to do a scene in one or two takes. Although committed to the project, Steve often arrived on the set without even knowing his lines and would infuriate Jackie by spending a good deal of time in the restroom.

Jackie was consistently exasperated. Steve seemed consistently indifferent. Steve was chagrined that Blake no longer was directing the film and felt he was doing his job merely by showing up at the designated hour. Perhaps at that time he was incapable of giving the calibre of performance that he would deliver several times in later years.

When Jackie and I spoke privately of Steve's

lack of focus on anything but his wheels, I discovered Jackie to be more compassionate and understanding than he frequently appeared. But Jackie was a great role-player. Perhaps he enjoyed the guise of a noble elder statesman during intimate conversations.

One day, however, Jackie exploded, resulting in an incident I shall never forget. I had special bathrobes designed for both men to wear and keep in their dressing rooms. As Steve labored over his lines at rehearsal, Jackie stormed off to his dressing room. Wearing his bathrobe, he drove away in a golf cart, leaving the set and probably the entire movie.

I had to think quickly. I knew that our stage was a fair distance from the dressing rooms. I called the wardrobe department and told them to remove all vestiges of Jackie's clothes. This would give me time to talk to Jackie. I knew that his clothes were custom tailored, which indicated he wanted to appear well-dressed when going out. He wouldn't want The Great One ever to be thought of as unkempt.

I sped to Jackie's dressing room and found him fuming in his bathrobe, venting his volcanic rage at the absent Steve.

"He doesn't just go to the head once," he shouted, sounding like *The Honeymooners'* Ralph Kramden yelling at Ed Norton. "He goes to the head ten times while we're trying to get one scene done!"

I spent the next couple of hours appeasing, pleading, cajoling, and even crying. Finally, Jackie agreed to go back.

Vastly relieved, I asked, "Is there anything I can do to show my appreciation?"

"Of course there is," Jackie replied immediately.

Jackie admitted to having a phobia about going to the barber shop. He wanted the shop to come to him. He wanted us to bring his favorite hair stylist to the set once a week. The price was sixty-five dollars a trim. The hair stylist turned out to be soft-spoken, delicate Jay Sebring, who was the force behind a spectacular array of hair products. He would become tragically famous as one of the victims of the infamous Manson Family's murderous rampage in 1969.

I asked Jay what made him so successful. He said, "I recognize the importance of the back of the head. Most people don't think it's as important as the front, but it is. When you watch a man walk away, that impression may be even more important than when you watch him approaching."

Many of my memories of *Soldier in the Rain* are positive. It was one of the first films of Tony Bill, who would have a successful career as actor and director. And Tuesday Weld, rumored to be a difficult talent, was cooperative and hard-working. She and Jackie had some lovely scenes together. I think being with a legend like Jackie and a rising star like Steve made Tuesday want to demonstrate the height of her professionalism, much as, years later, Debra Winger would be her most professional when Jack Nicholson was on the set of *Terms of Endearment*.

Time has a way of extending curative powers. Certainly, there were trying days working with both Jackie and Steve. But in looking back, I've mellowed in my judgment. For decades Jackie revealed his extraordinary talents, and he gave so many hours of pleasure to the world. He even proved capable of showing respect to others. He signed an autographed picture to me, with the words "To the producer" underlined several times.

Soldier in the Rain did not elevate Jackie to the top pantheon of top movie stars. He would almost reach his coveted goal with the *Smokey and the*

Bandit series, although even those movies were considered box-office vehicles for Burt Reynolds rather than Jackie.

Steve always had a group of followers. Both men and women were anxious to spin wheels with him. They felt protective of him because he always seemed to be living in another world, a world that he definitely preferred to the real one. Skeptical and suspicious of people in the industry, he was most comfortable spinning wheels. But his legacy of films continues to be favorably reexamined. As long as "cool" remains a desirable adjective, Steve McQueen is assured of a coveted place in the movie galaxy.

Steve McQueen (left) and Jackie Gleason allow themselves a smile as they size each other up between takes on *Soldier in the Rain*. (Photograph by William Claxton)

17

Terms of Endearment

~

My life with Shirley MacLaine can be recorded as travels in time. And, with Shirley, no title could be more appropriate.

Shirley is a ceaselessly fascinating woman—searching within herself, questing for soulmates, and, as we all know, forming strong opinions. She's inquisitive, humorous, dramatic, and, when she feels cornered or betrayed, she's absolutely fierce. My admiration for her is boundless.

The first stop in my MacLaine Book of Memories begins with one of those legendary coincidences that might have been borrowed from a backstage musical. In 1954, Erin-Jo and I had tickets for *The Pajama Game* on Broadway. Sitting next to us was my former boss Hal B. Wallis. A dreaded announcement was issued prior to curtain time. The musical's star, Carol Haney, was ill and would be replaced that evening by her understudy.

I moaned. Erin-Jo moaned. Wallis permitted himself a most baleful moan. A symphony of moans echoed throughout the theater. By the end of the evening, they had turned into rhapsodic cheers.

The show had no single number that demonstrated how understudy Shirley MacLaine captivated the disgruntled audience. It was the totality of Shirley's personality—whimsical, saucy, romantic, wisecracking, pixie-ish yet womanly. Her performance that night was her initiation to a stardom that still lasts.

Hal accompanied us back to our apartment, where Erin-Jo prepared a light supper. I encouraged him to sign Shirley to a contract immediately. She had been dynamic on the stage and, I felt certain, she would be dynamic on the screen.

And so Shirley came to Hollywood with a Hal Wallis contract. These two stubborn individuals were fated not to get along. Shirley lacked the blatant sexuality that Hal found attractive in women, and she had enough self-esteem to avoid the male-female games that endeared some actresses to moguls.

Hal misused her unique talents, consigning her to decorative roles. Her strongest early challenges, such as her Oscar-nominated goodtime girl

in 1959's *Some Came Running*, were made outside his fold. And Shirley, justifiably, never takes kindly to having her talents misused. She got out of her contract, but not without a severance of whatever goodwill remained between her and Wallis.

The next image in my MacLaine kaleidoscope is in the early 1960s, before Audrey Hepburn signed for *Breakfast at Tiffany's*. Shirley called me, so desperate to play Holly Golightly that she gladly would test for the part. But we discovered that our starting date conflicted with *Two Loves*.

Shirley, a woman of resolve and judgment, honored her MGM commitment. Her test for Holly Golightly was never made. We would meet again through the years, always with warmth and respect. But we never worked together until two decades later, and the result would be a hallmark of both our careers.

In the early 1980s, a man with the wonderful Texas name of Wid Slick strode into my Dallas office. We were casual acquaintances, but Wid always expressed a high opinion of my work. A mysterious man, Wid never revealed much about himself.

Wid had just taken an option on *Terms of Endearment*, a novel by Texas's favorite son Larry McMurtry, who had written *The Last Picture Show* and would later add *Lonesome Dove* to his credits.

I read the book right away and told Wid that I would be delighted to work with him. The book's leading character, Houston dowager Aurora Greenway, appealed to me. She was imperious but vulnerable, ostensibly selfish yet capable of generosity, outwardly prim but filled with passion.

I had one person in mind for the part: Shirley MacLaine.

For *Terms of Endearment* to succeed, Aurora

had to be played by someone fearless. I had never known Shirley to be afraid of anything. Cautious, yes, on rare occasions. But never fearful. She also possesses an edginess essential to Aurora, who was not always the easiest person to spend an hour with.

Above all, Shirley is a caring soul. Although her one marriage to producer Steve Parker was unhappy, she dearly loves their daughter Satchi and would certainly understand Aurora's attachment to her daughter Emma. Shirley tries to love every character she plays, whether it's the spurned elevator girl of 1960's *The Apartment*, the happy hookers of 1963's *Irma La Douce* and 1968's *Sweet Charity*, or the bewildered mother of 1977's *The Turning Point*. Some actors separate themselves from their roles. Not Shirley. She cares about them, and she makes us care about them.

My choice of director was Daniel Petrie, a fine human being with a knack for such character-driven films as *A Raisin in the Sun*, *Resurrection*, and *Fort Apache, The Bronx*. Unfortunately, he has never received the acclaim he so richly deserves.

Not long after we optioned *Terms of Endearment*, Larry McMurtry came to see us, his manner curt and businesslike. Jennifer Jones, widow of David O. Selznick and now married to Norton Simon, had made a substantial cash offer for the book, planning to play Aurora herself. He had no intention of signing our option. We were stunned. But all pleading or displays of righteous indignation were useless.

Eventually we allowed him to forego the option, but I warned him that Jennifer Jones would never make the film. She had created a sensation in 1943 as the gentle saint of *The Song of Bernadette*, but she was no longer active in filmmaking. She was involved in preserving her persona—that of a

Marty counsels Shirley MacLaine, who won an Oscar for the role of Aurora Greenway in *Terms of Endearment*.

vague, whimsical child-woman. Absolutely wrong for the judgmental, decisive Aurora, Jennifer was at one with violins. Aurora was a rasping horn.

Just as McMurtry was leaving, Wid uttered what I consider a classic Texan line in its brevity and resonance: "Rest assured that if you come back to us, you will not be welcomed."

That experience was a major disappointment and a sharp blow. With *Terms of Endearment*, I felt we had that rare project that culminates in both strong box-office and numerous awards. But those of us in the movie business get over grief quickly. We have to.

And now let's jump-cut to 1982. I am filming *Waltz Across Texas* in Midland, Texas, starring my goddaughter Anne Archer, her husband Terry Jastrow and the wonderful actress Mary Kay Place.

Mary Kay had completed her work on the film, and she and Erin-Jo had spent the day antique-shopping in nearby Odessa. They stopped off for coffee at a pancake house midway between Odessa and Midland. Mary Kay mentioned that there was a project coming up that she would love to do.

"It's based on a book by Larry McMurtry," Mary Kay said. "I have a very good friend who's really trying to get it off the ground."

"What's the name of the book?" asked Erin-Jo, who of course knew of my fondness for a certain McMurtry property.

"*Terms of Endearment*, and my friend is Jim Brooks," she said, referring to television wizard James Brooks, responsible for such hit comedy series as *The Mary Tyler Moore Show*, *Taxi*, *Rhoda*, and *Phyllis*.

Mary Kay then added, "I really think Jim needs Martin on this movie. He's having trouble financing it. Martin could be of help."

"Martin loves that book!" Erin-Jo said. "He's been wanting to film it ever since he read it."

"Where is Martin?" asked Mary Kay.

"In California."

"Go call him. Call him right now."

And so, from a roadside Texas pancake house, Erin-Jo made one of the most important phone calls of my later career.

"Mary Kay says for you to call Jim Brooks at Paramount. He's trying to make a movie of *Terms of Endearment*."

It was almost two P.M. in Los Angeles. By five P.M., I had met with Jim to discuss the film with him and was officially co-producer of *Terms of Endearment*.

This was an amazing demonstration of trust and confidence between two men who had known each other for less than three hours. We trusted each other's instincts and judgments. We agreed on all major aspects of the production.

One agreement completely solidified our relationship. We both thought the redoubtable matriarch Aurora Greenway could be played by only one actress, Shirley MacLaine.

Jim not only had written the screenplay but was convinced that only he could direct it. The Hollywood moguls were not so certain, this being his first try at movie directing. Jim was wounded by their attitude, which he felt dismissed his vast work on television.

Paramount had expressed interest in *Terms*, only to refuse his budget figures. Jim would allow no detour to his path. He asked me to study the budget and see if it could be reduced. I was glad to do so. I knew that with Jim, a reduced budget would never mean a reduction in quality.

Paramount had put our film in turnaround, which permitted us to seek other financing, with Paramount retaining the right to match any other studio's offer. This led us to MGM and an agreement with studio chief David Begelman, a controversial and ultimately tragic figure. And then, as we moved our screenplay and our ideas to Metro, we heard that David Begelman had been deposed.

His replacement was Freddie Fields. To Jim and me, Fields issued a stunning statement: "Leave the studio. Anyone who wants to make a movie with the girl dying at the end will not make a movie for us."

This, from the man who in 1977 produced *Looking for Mr. Goodbar*, which ended with Diane Keaton's character slashed to death.

Eventually a company that had worked with Jim to great acclaim, the Mary Tyler Moore Company, helped with the funding that allowed us to go back to Paramount.

The filming of *Terms of Endearment* was in many ways a test of endurance. I never left the set during the filming. Jim had chosen an enormous emotional load for his first film as a director, and he was not one to be flexible in his decisions. Sometimes his lack of experience showed, and he was rescued by more experienced crew members, which aided the film but wounded his pride.

He and I had several confrontations, and he seemed dismayed that I would dare question his decisions. He wanted to film in Houston. I wanted Dallas, which had greater manpower and more proficient technical crews. But Jim wanted Houston, and Houston it was.

Shirley was my chief concern. She and Jim were having sharp clashes regarding her interpretation of Aurora. Finally she walked away from the set toward her dressing room, and I could sense that she was about to make a radical decision. Through tears, she said it would be best to stop while the filming was still in its early stages and that she was calling her manager.

I put my arms around her as her body shook.

"Shirley, how many films have you made?"

"Thirty-five," she said, her voice muffled by tears.

"And how many pictures has James Brooks made?" I queried.

"Why, he hasn't even made a single movie yet! This is his first," she said, her tears drying.

"Well, then, who should be more professional?"

We sat for a while, and then Shirley agreed to return to the set.

"But I'm not going to talk to anyone!" she declared.

"You don't have to," I ventured. "Just do what Spencer Tracy did."

"What did he do?" she asked, intrigued.

"Just say your lines."

Shirley's apprehension lessened when I agreed to fly her favorite manicurist to Houston. That manicure wound up costing the company $750. But Shirley proved to be well worth what seemed like the world's most expensive nail polish. She, Jim Brooks, and Jack Nicholson all won Oscars.

Brooks thanked me personally for my work with Shirley. And fourteen years later, when I wrote to congratulate him on the success of *As Good As It Gets*, he wrote back a charming, warm letter.

Shirley was not the only strong-willed actress involved in the turbulent *Terms*. When I first saw Debra Winger, we fell into each other's arms. Everything I had heard about her alluded to her toughness, but in person, she looked like a waif, like Hans Christian Andersen's Little Match Girl.

Looks were deceiving. Debra was definitely tough.

Following *An Officer and a Gentleman*, a film she loathed, she was at the peak of her popularity, and the entire company anticipated how Shirley and Debra might react to each other. It was expected that these two strong personalities would both seek superiority, particularly when working

Shirley MacLaine, Danny DeVito (with Marty standing behind him) and Jack Nicholson all gave Houston something to talk about during filming of *Terms of Endearment*.

with Jack Nicholson, cast as the randy astronaut who romances Aurora.

Much has been written about the Shirley/Debra combat zone, and some of it has been exaggerated. Instead of clawing at each other to be first in Jack's esteem, they were on good behavior whenever he was present. Shirley had known Jack through his friendship with her brother Warren Beatty and was determined that he respect her on a professional level. Jack wound up a peacemaker in the two actresses' war of wills.

Shirley remained a dominant figure, while Debra often was irritable.

One memorably hot and clammy day, she came on the set and announced, "I wish I were not working today—or ever."

Her personal life was in an upheaval at the moment, and she was making strong moves towards the attractive Nebraska governor, Bob Kerrey. When we shot scenes in Lincoln, Nebraska, she spent many hours in the Governor's Mansion, always coming back more relaxed.

Marty is dissolved into laughter by a teasing Debra Winger on the set of *Terms of Endearment*.

She's a daring, risk-taking actress, but her career has been hindered by a selection of weak roles in such films as *Wilder Napalm* and *Forget Paris*. She made a mistake when she left the cast of the hit comedy *A League of Their Own* to protest what she called the "stunt casting" of Madonna. Debra often feels that her judgment is better than anyone's. But the trajectory of her career often proved otherwise.

Through it all, Jack Nicholson was a source of serenity. He's one of the easiest actors to work with, provided you understand his necessities. He loves music and always wanted his vast collection of CDs at his fingertips. And, being a passionate Lakers fan, he naturally felt he should be excused when he desired to see his favorite basketball team. You also had to understand that Jack abhors small talk. People on the set soon learned not even to attempt a quick chat with him. But he was capable of wisdom and compassion.

On one occasion, my nerves were frayed by certain occurrences on the set. While filming in Houston, one of the crew had made advances to a neighbor's teenage daughter. Finally, the neighbor agreed to keep the daughter away from the set. And, in general, the combination of Shirley, Debra, and Jim was combustible. Jack knew everything that went on and was sympathetic to my plight. He would say to me in the most soothing tones possible, "One day at a time, Marty . . . One day at a time."

He showed his kindness in unexpected ways. Our Houston location centered on one large house. But neighbors' homes were used in some shots, and the owners were understandably fearful of any injury to their property. One geriatric lady had lived in her house all her adult life and was particularly apprehensive. Erin-Jo sat next to her and calmed her fears.

Jack completely understood the woman's concern. After every take, he would turn and wave to her, flashing his finest Jack Nicholson smile. That's not the sort of gesture you might expect from Jack, but he was completely sincere.

Regardless of the filming experience, I have warm memories of *Terms of Endearment* mingled with professional, artistic pride.

Co-producing an Oscar-winning blockbuster like *Terms of Endearment* while in my early seventies exhilarated me. The film broke all contemporary rules. It was character-driven rather than effects-driven, and its two main characters were women. This, at a time when Hollywood movies were almost exclusively male-dominated. And, of course, it had a sad ending.

The movie was a champion. Erin-Jo and I went to Los Angeles for the Academy Awards and visited shops and restaurants we had frequented through the years. Warm regards from friends on both coasts assured me of longstanding relationships with the entertainment community.

And I smile with great affection whenever I read the inscription Shirley sent me with a copy of her memoirs, *Out on a Limb*:

"Darling Marty, for your compassion, understanding and professionalism, thank you for being you . . . What an experience!"

An experience, it was. It brought my MacLaine Mosaic to full circle. I was there for *The Pajama Game*, and I was there for *Terms of Endearment*. I wouldn't have missed either experience.

Shirley is radiantly articulate, with interests beyond her career. She can be enormous fun and is wise enough to know that not everyone takes her truth-seeking seriously. This realization doesn't deter her one bit. When her mind is set, nothing in this or any other world deters Shirley.

Jack Nicholson may look mischievous, but he was an anchor of dignity on the set of *Terms of Endearment*.

18

Dallas Days

~

It was the only time I saw Jack Warner smile with real tenderness.

Before returning to California from England, where I had been head of European production for Warner Bros., one of my last continental visits was to Jack, at his villa in the south of France. He told me he was selling the studio to Seven Arts. Jack had been one of the most tight-fisted of executives, but the mellow Jack whom I now encountered gave me sufficient severance.

I thanked him for telling me, and my mind flew back a quarter of a century to our nightly ritual when I worked at Warner Bros.

"Let's put out the lights, J. L., let's put out the lights," I said.

His smile was soft and lingering, and I knew he was remembering, too. I think it's significant that his last personal production for the studio was *Camelot*, a story of faded dreams in a mythical setting of fabled splendor.

Hollywood is not the sort of town that allows you to grow old gracefully. Moviemaking has always

been a young person's profession, and I did not want to grow old in Hollywood. I knew it was time for a drastic change.

I was still offered scripts to produce, and studio chiefs still returned my calls. But none of those scripts stirred my creative juices. The material unnerved me with its sexual promiscuity, violence, and defamation of language. In both my youth and adulthood, I never joined a club where I thought loathsome jokes might be heard. In my films, I never objected to sexual innuendo, which can be sophisticated and entertaining, but I've always believed that sexuality should be private. The movies were making it more public than ever.

Agencies tried to lure me with lucrative offers. But at sixty years of age, I wanted a new vocation and a new location. I never thought of retiring. I'd had rewarding times, both personally and professionally, in New York and Los Angeles, and I sought new horizons.

I did not seek to give up moviemaking. I just wanted to change bases, and I knew where I was

Marty with the brilliant character actor Richard Farnsworth, on the set of *Sylvester* near El Paso, Texas. Facing cancer, Farnsworth shot himself in October, 2000. Marty remembers his "purity as an actor and as a human being."

going. Erin-Jo is Texas-born with fond memories of Dallas, where she spent some of her growing-up years. I had read a great deal about the Sunbelt and knew that Dallas was thriving.

The thought of starting over in a new locale was exhilarating. We settled comfortably in our new hometown and found the people warm, friendly, and forthright. Texans truly speak in "terms of endearment."

I became involved in the advancement of Texas filmmaking. There was no movie company in Dallas in the early 1970s, and I spent hours with Gov. Preston Smith, nurturing the newly formed Texas Film Commission and advancing the USA Film Festival, which started in Dallas in 1970.

Gregory Peck, a truly lovely human being, was a guest at one of the first film festivals. When an audience member asked if there was one particular role he would like to play, he immediately responded, "I'd love to play Gen. MacArthur, but I haven't been asked."

The audience applauded vigorously. Greg's demeanor always commanded respect, making him an ideal choice for a military figure.

I knew that Frank McCarthy was planning the film biography of Gen. MacArthur. I had known Frank ever since he was publicity manager for George Abbott, and he and I had worked together promoting *Brother Rat*. I immediately called him, emphasizing the enthusiastic audience response when Greg said he'd love to be MacArthur.

That night Greg knew he was a candidate. A week later, we received a late-night call. Greg's unmistakable velvet voice announced, "This is Gen. Douglas MacArthur. I'd like to speak to Martin."

Unfortunately *MacArthur* was not the career highlight it should have been. But Greg got to play a complex character, one whom he loved despite their political differences. And he was superb in it.

My own first Texas films were inexpensive features, primarily made to test the Dallas talent pool. One film was budgeted at $84,000. Another came in at $102,000. Their titles were *Keep My Grave Open* and *Don't Look Back*, but they were steeped in mythic folklore rather than true horror. My name is not on either of those films.

Those initial movies were filmed in the lovely city of Jefferson, Texas, 160 miles from Dallas and with a population of two thousand. We bought a weekend home in Jefferson, a Texas landmark called The Manse, built in the 1840s. Aside from having Jefferson as a weekend retreat, we visited Hughes Springs in East Texas. Erin-Jo had spent part of her growing-up years there, and I loved seeing the park where she remembered spending happy hours.

In promoting the Texas Film Commission and counseling aspiring filmmakers, I visited cities in other states, all of which reinforced my loyalty to Dallas.

I spoke with Georgia's then-governor Jimmy Carter, who gave his approval for a television series, *The Atlanta Force*, to be made in that city. Unfortunately, banks were not forthcoming.

He then asked if I had any recommendations for his appearance on television.

"What kind of suit are you wearing on TV?" I asked.

"Oh, blue," he said, a little puzzled.

"Give yourself added plumage," I advised. "Wear a gray suit with a blue shirt and a colorful tie. Increase the pitch of your tie."

Whenever I saw President Carter addressing the nation, I would smile, remembering the earnest governor who wanted to know how to look good on television.

I went to Little Rock to converse with Gov. Bill Clinton. He used all his personal persuasiveness to convince the Texas Film Commission to join forces with Arkansas, but to no avail. Mr. Clinton is a genuine movie buff, and I would not be surprised if he winds up in an executive position within the movie colony.

Sadly, the climate was not favorable for regional film production. Some Hollywood figures had already come to Dallas with lavish plans, only to leave abruptly when immediate funding was not forthcoming. Investors were interested in agriculture, cattle, and chemicals. They were interested in movies, but their interest did not extend to investments.

I was heartsick. I've always loved to keep busy. Retirement did not appeal to me because I've been blessed with an abundance of energy. One evening in Jefferson, Erin-Jo and I were discussing our love of Texas and our understanding of its reluctance to finance film production. Late that night, I felt her hand on my shoulder and her voice in my ear.

"Martin, you have a latent talent that you have not yet used," she said.

"What do you mean?"

"The law."

"Oh, Erin-Jo, I passed the New York bar exam in 1936. This is 1976. I haven't touched a law book in forty years. There's no chance, there's no way . . ."

"Why don't you try?"

And try, I did.

At the age of sixty-five, not having looked at a law book in four decades, I found myself sitting in Southern Methodist University's George Underwood Law Library, studying sixteen courses to pass the Texas bar. I started by studying two hours a day, then four, then eight.

I went to Austin for the bar exam. Looking back, I realize how bold I was. On the bar exam's last question, my answer was simple: "I cannot write anymore. I hope the reader will realize that I know the answer, as I have known other answers. But I cannot write another sentence."

I passed the bar exam. Much to my amazement, the Chief Justice of the Supreme Court of Texas asked for my autograph. Many times through the years, I had stepped aside as fans begged autographs from their idols. Now I gladly gave mine.

Passing the bar exam after not cracking a law book for forty years gave me vitality and curiosity. I had lived in show business for four decades, and I wanted to expand. It was a great feeling.

I talked my way into the office of legendary district attorney Henry Wade, the noted legal eagle who had convicted Jack Ruby.

When he asked, "Why in the world are you interested in joining the district attorney's office?"

I mischievously replied, "Because it would make a great movie."

I became assistant district attorney and Henry Wade's personal assistant as well.

It was a wonderful period of my life. I had never been a great fan of lawyers, finding some to be insufferably pompous as well as guilty of deeds they would be litigious about. Yet I loved working with a group of 104 district attorneys, most in their early thirties. I was refreshed, and my mind was alert. I had never felt so energized. Walking up the courthouse steps with those young district attorneys was one of the most exciting times of my life.

I had been wise to choose not to grow old in Hollywood.

I was considered something of a curio, and curiosity was heightened when a voice echoed through the corridors of the County Courthouse, saying "Mr. Gregory Peck is on the phone, calling for Mr. Martin Jurow."

Henry Wade was quiet and reserved, also shrewd and wily. He had no sympathy for Jack Ruby, whom he had sent to trial. We had lunch together at least twice a week, and I would enjoy watching him cut his cigars. They were short, stubby cigars, like the ones John Ford smoked, and he would often chew on them. He never revealed much about himself, but he was capable of warmth. I felt that he hoped I would arrange for a book to be written about him, but the book never materialized.

I spent two and one-half years with Henry Wade, and although I enjoyed the experience, the financial rewards were minimal. Eventually I decided to take advantage of other offers. I left with his blessing.

One of Erin-Jo's and my dearest friends is Dallas philanthropist and benefactor Ruth Collins Sharp Altshuler. Chairman of Southern Methodist

Sally Sharp in *The End of August*, produced by Marty Jurow, a film based on Kate Chopin's early feminist book, *The Awakening*.

University's board of trustees, she's on the national boards of the Salvation Army and the United Way. Her friends were as varied as Lord Mountbatten, George Cukor, Gene Kelly, and Ginger Rogers.

Ruth's daughter Sally, a talented young woman with a strong interest in the arts, was mesmerized by Kate Chopin's haunting early-twentieth-century novel *The Awakening*, which had

stoked some of the first fires of American feminism. Sally and Ruth said that if I would produce a film of Chopin's novel, they would help find the funding. Our film version of *The Awakening* was called *The End of August*. It was shot in Mobile, Alabama, with a distinguished cast that included Sally Sharp, Lilia Skala, David Marshall Grant, Kathleen Widdoes, Paul Roebling, Paul Shenar,

Mark-Linn Baker, and Saundra Santiago. The movie received strong reviews and was a great success at the Deauville Film Festival.

I returned to filmmaking under the most harmonious of circumstances. I've often wished that Sally would have continued acting. She is now the mother of three and devotes much time to the Salvation Army, filming a superb documentary about the charity organization.

My next film, *Waltz Across Texas*, starred our goddaughter Anne Archer, daughter of our friend Marjorie Lord, and Anne's husband, golf star Terry Jastrow. The supporting cast included Mary Kay Place and Richard Farnsworth. It was shot entirely in Terry's hometown of Midland, Texas, then a booming oil town. Within one week, we had ample funding. Had we come to Midland even six months later, we would not have been able to raise money. The oil business is that precarious.

And it was in Midland that Erin-Jo had the fateful discussion with Mary Kay Place, which realized my dream of making a movie version of the novel *Terms of Endearment* by Larry McMurtry.

After the adventure of *Terms of Endearment*, detailed in the preceding chapter, veteran producer Ray Stark, maker of such films as *Funny Girl*, *The Way We Were*, and *The Night of the Iguana*, called upon me to produce *Sylvester*, a delightful girl-loves-horse movie starring Melissa Gilbert and, once again, the sublime character actor Richard Farnsworth, who would be lauded in 1999 for *The Straight Story*. At the request of Rosemary Benton, wife of Don Benton, minister of the Lovers Lane Methodist Church in Dallas, I helped produce *Papa Was a Preacher*.

I returned to the position of executive producer for a tribute to John F. Kennedy, the film

Anne Archer and her husband and leading man
Terry Jastrow in *Waltz Across Texas*.

Anne Archer and Terry Jastrow in Midland.

shown at the Sixth Floor Museum in Dallas, the memorial to JFK at the site of the Texas Schoolbook Depository. Dallas documentary filmmakers Allen and Cynthia Mondell were instrumental in its remarkable success. The museum has attracted visitors from around the world.

New opportunities arrived, each one seeming like an early Christmas gift. One day in 1986, Kermit Hunter, dean of the Meadows School of Arts at SMU, came by for a visit.

"You have so much more knowledge about filmmaking than anyone else in the city," he said. "Why not teach a course?"

Just as in my early years I had longed to produce, I now longed to teach. I had been thinking this over before Kermit's visit and suggested a course in business opportunities within the world of entertainment.

I taught the course for ten years. *Goodbye, Mr. Chips* is one of my favorite movies, and now I got the chance to be a Mr. Chips. My students were fascinated by Old Hollywood and respectful of the talent that was involved.

The same year I began my teaching career, I began a radio show at KAAM. I once visited the local ASCAP offices in the Dallas suburb of Plano. In the same building was the KAAM radio station. After a quick meeting of the minds with the station's program director Danny Owen, I began narrating a radio show, *Martin Jurow of Show Business*, which ran for ten years, and was rewarded with many letters and phone calls. People often stop Erin-Jo and me and repeat verbatim an anecdote I had spun from my fifty years in the entertainment

Marty discussing *Papa Was a Preacher* with Robert Pine (left).

Marty (center) in a quiet moment with Melissa Gilbert and Richard Farnsworth on the set of *Sylvester*.

Marty with Audrey Hepburn—a reunion in Dallas when she was honored by the USA Film Festival in 1991.

business. Those fifty years seem like ten at the most. When you love what you do, time moves quickly.

Early in the 1990s, I met one of the brightest men I've ever encountered, Dallas lawyer Stephen P. Jarchow. He came to me with the idea for Regent

Entertainment, a mini-studio that finances and produces films. We met regularly for much of the decade, discussing various aspects of the movie industry. I served as senior advisor to Regent, and Steve shepherded the company to great international success with *Gods and Monsters*, with Oscar-nominated performances by Ian McKellen and Lynn Redgrave.

As I look back, I realize that the world also looks back with fondness. Almost every year, film-makers rediscover the classics of William Shake-speare, Jane Austen, Thomas Hardy, and Henry James. I think of Broadway's new version of *The Scarlet Pimpernel* and its revivals of *Guys and Dolls*, *Annie Get Your Gun*, *The King and I*, *Show Boat*,

Years after Marty sent Van Johnson (center) to Hollywood, where he became a bobbysoxers' favorite, they enjoyed a reunion in Dallas at an art exhibit of Van's paintings in the early 1980s. At right is Mary John, a Northwood Institute organizer.

Marty and Erin-Jo with Audrey Hepburn in Dallas. An evening filled with memories.

Erin Jurow with Duke.

The Music Man, and *Kiss Me, Kate*, which won a bouquet of Tony Awards in 2000. And not a season goes by without a community theater production of *Oklahoma!* or *My Fair Lady*.

I had the good fortune to be involved in movie production during the studio system's golden era. When I see today's movies, I note the names of Paramount, Warner Bros., Universal, 20th Century Fox, Columbia, and Disney. These corporations function in ways that the old tycoons could not have foreseen. But their names are the same, and I am thrilled to see that their corporate entities still exist after so many years.

I remain a frequent moviegoer and enjoy much of what I see. I consider *Schindler's List* a masterpiece and *Titanic* a great piece of popular entertainment. It was a thrill watching Julia Roberts emerge as an actress and future star in *Mystic Pizza*, just as it was gratifying to witness Tom Hanks successfully take risks in *Forrest Gump*.

My life has been an odyssey in which I used

both my law degree and my fascination with the entertainment world, a love that began eighty years ago with those Brooklyn vaudeville shows. I followed my dream and ended up with a wealth of human experience. I was never fired from any job, never prodded to leave. And I made good on a pledge I made to myself many decades ago: I never took the subway to work.

I really have had a wonderful life. I feel surrounded by a circle of love, strengthened by our daughter Erin, our sister-in-law Mae, and our grandson Will Eliscu, who is involved in the production of movies. Will is a keen talent and an excellent artist.

And always there is Erin-Jo. Even now, after fifty-seven years of marriage, we love to sit together and talk about the day's events. When we reminisce, I see the faces of Frank, Marlon, Elvis, Sammy, Audrey, Kate, Shirley MacLaine, Gary Cooper, Jack Nicholson, Jack Lemmon, Burt, Kirk, Steve McQueen, Ava, and Lucy and Desi. It has been a remarkable odyssey, and we can't wait to see what tomorrow will bring.

Grandson William Guinn Eliscu. (Photograph by Paul Abel)

Martin Jurow is now retired and lives with his wife Erin-Jo and daughter Erin in Dallas. (Photograph by John Bird)

Index

J. D. Palasek

PHILIP WUNTCH, a lifelong Texan, is also a longtime movie fan. He made his hobby his life's work when he joined the staff of *The Dallas Morning News* as an entertainment writer in 1969. He has been film critic there since 1974. He makes his home in Dallas and still loves going to the movies with his wife Mimi.

6.30.59
Fugitive Kind at Milton

To my friends Ellen-Jo & Marty
Best wishes 64 Dong Kingman

Kingman

filming of "Fugitive Kind"
at milton   June 30-1959
To my friends Allen To & Martin
Dore [illegible] [illegible]